COVER IMAGE

"Untitled"

Alicia Starr Ryan

2007, Mixed Media

10 inches by 16 inches

in situ

a collection of literary and visual arts from the iowa city area

PUBLISHED BY

A subsidiary of Gannett Co. Inc.
1725 N. Dodge St., Iowa City, IA 52245
www.insituic.com

Printed and bound by Goodfellow Printing,
Iowa City, Iowa

Copyright 2007 by "In situ."
All rights retained by the authors and artists.
First edition
ISBN No. 0-9712727-2-7

Acknowledgements

PROJECT DIRECTOR
Emily Hagemann

OPERATING COMMITTEE
Dan Brown
Jeff Charis-Carlson
Alicia Starr Ryan

DESIGN AND PRODUCTION
Alicia Starr Ryan
Emily Hagemann

ONLINE EDITOR
Patrick Riepe

REVIEW COMMITTEE
Jason Bengtson
Dan Brown
Jeff Charis-Carlson
Anne Craig
Emily Hagemann
John Hudson
Sandra Hudson
Alicia Starr Ryan
Deanna Truman

Although university professors frown upon citing Wikipedia as a source, the online, public encyclopedia still provides the best definition for "in situ" (in si'too):

"An artifact being in situ is critical to the interpretation of that artifact and, consequently, to the culture which formed it. Once an artifact's 'find-site' has been recorded, the artifact can then be moved for conservation, further interpretation and display. An artifact that is not discovered in situ is considered out of context and will not provide an accurate picture of the associated culture. However, the out of context artifact can provide scientists with an example of types and locations of in situ artifacts yet to be discovered."

We've chosen the Latin term as the title for this sure-to-be annual collection of locally produced visual and literary arts because of the multiple echoes the term has in different fields:

- In art, it refers to the manner in which you do the work;
- In archaeology, it refers to an artifact that has not been moved from its original place;
- In architecture, it means construction that is carried out on the building site using raw materials;
- In biology, it means to examine the phenomenon exactly in place where it occurs;
- In linguistics, it refers to an element that is pronounced in the position where it is interpreted; and
- In law, it often refers to a statement's literal meaning.

When we first proposed "In situ," we decided to declare it a success if it attracted 200 submissions. With local writers and artists submitting nearly twice that number, the collection has exceeded our already high expectations. The 96 works of art presented here provide a representative sampling of local poetry, photography, painting, sculpture, collage, essay, fiction, journalism and oratory. It's the distilled essence of one year in our local creative economy.

Plans are already under way for next year's "In situ." Keep visiting www.insituic.com for updates and for information about this year's featured writers and artists. And thank you for helping to make the Iowa City area such a supportive artistic community.

— *Dan Brown, Jeff Charis-Carlson, Emily Hagemann and Alicia Starr Ryan.*

in situ

table of contents

The Sublime	Dan Campion	8
Lessons from Pigg Farm	Alan Brody	9
Teaching English in War Time	Mary Vermillion	17
The Van Pool's Grace	L. Ward McFarlane	18
The Map	Tamara Batie	25
The Best Things Happen Slowly	Andy Douglas	26
Geography Song	John Birkbeck	28
Small World	Jeff Charis-Carlson	29
Iowa	Nick Smith	33
Horseback Writer	Adele Bonney	34
The Painter, the Sculptor, the Poet	Linda Bolton	35
A Variation on a Theme IV	Chris Kilgore	36
The Hired Man	Fran Gruenhaupt	40
Sons and Daughters	Terry Wahls	43
Workaday	Joseph M. Petrick	45
Transgression	Corinne Stanley	52
The Cereal Aisle	Mary Vermillion	53
Lauds	Liz Lynn Miller	56
Psychedelia	Gerine Tenold	57
Centers	Shauna Banning	58
The Woods of Fall	Jason Bengtson	59
Menu	Liz Lynn Miller	62
To a Woman's Skinny Soul	Linda N. Woito	63
The Immovable Object vs. The Unstoppable Force	Chris Kilgore	64
Jumah	Spring Ulmer	70
Leave This Thermostat at Seventy-two Degrees	Adam Hahn	74
Redhorse Revelry	Nick Compton	78
Requiem for Jim's Rig	Rick Zollo	80
2537	Peter Feldstein	81
Arcadia Schooner	Barry Sharp	82
Broken Bottles	Andrew Whitters	83
Chopper Teapot	Jason Messier	84
Early Spring	Marcia Wegman	85

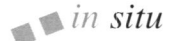 *in situ*

table of contents

Blossoms, Tree, Oregon Coast	Kenn Hubel	86
Body of Christ, Save Me	Rita Svoboda Tomanek	87
Ascent	Laura Young	88
Field	Craig Albright	89
Matt Lyvers	Changes	90
Jan Krieger	Emma and Harley	91
Dance	Ramon Lim	92
Glowing Trumpet	Dale Phillips	93
New Elation 2	Patricia Knox	94
Musical Truth	Brittany Noethen	95
Only Echoes	Cheryl Jacobsen	96
Dreams Done: Looking Ahead	Garth Conley	97
Rub A Dub Dub	Connie Roberts	98
Eastern Iowa Landscape	Gordon Kellenberger	99
Domestic Extrusions	Tom Aprile	100
Anxiety	Elizabeth Roberts	101
Free Flow	Shirley Wyrick	102
Walking Back	Sophie Radl	103
Balances	Astrid Hilger Bennett	104
Tiamah 08	Paul Cork	105
Iowa River Sunset	Linda & Robert Scarth	106
Les Fleur	Bernice Gantz	107
Early Evening Sun	Zakery Neumann	108
California	Tonya Kehoe	109
One	Jason Strating	110
Treesphere	Melinda Kaune	111
Riding the Rails	Mindy Stukel	112
God & Chaos	The Bomb Shaman	113
Sherbert Posers	Nick Meister	114
Slim to None	Julie Fitzpatrick	115
Suspended DewDrops	Howard Cox	116
All Aboard Herky	Jeff McNutt	117
Dragonfly	Phyllis Lance	118

in situ

table of contents

Water Works	Howard Hinton Jr.	119
Early Morning Mist	Sue Hershberger	120
Tree	Mary Carson	121
The Cost of Freedom	Helen Thompson	122
The Wise Tree and the Foolish Bush	Carol Blomberg	124
A Hundred Acres	PJM Atkinson	128
Shopping with Zorro — Iowa City '58	Lois Muehl	129
Supernova	Frederik Norberg	135
Episode	Dan Campion	136
The Artist's Labcoat	Patrick McCue	137
Forza Roma	Kathryn Welsh	141
A Morning for Growing Older	Dannye Seager Frerichs	145
Why We Choose Who We Choose	Suzanne Cody	146
Mr. Drone	Nick Smith	151
Thick Skin	Krissy Dallmann	152
I Dun, Uhmannumb	Jonathan Starke	154
Warmth	Kate Miller	159
Messages Written, Never Mailed	Patricia Davis	160
Not Yet	Jean Murphy Rude	162
Exercise vs. Working Out: A Tongue-in-cheek Primer	JD Mendenhall	163
Nothing But A Smile For Mrs. Marken	Matthew Black	166
Wallace for President	Rick Zollo	167
Benediction In Spite Of	Jennifer R. Horn	173
Break in the Drought	Barbara J. Kalm	174
Mustache	Beverly Johlin	175
Mormon Trek Off Benton	Denise Tiffany	176
Widow in the Window	M.P. Sarabia	178
The Death of a Cat	William Ford	183
The Obstinate Conception	Jean Junis	184
As I Sit Here Thinking	Michael L. McNulty	185
The Barking Warrior	Mary Joanne Roberts	186
Biographies		188

Dan Campion

The Sublime

for David Yerkes

Afield in storms, Douglas tempted lightning.
Jim hit frostbite like black ice on slick roads.
I've swayed on ledges wearying to climb.
But you, David, ranged the manifold modes
Of the sublime.
                    Rushes of prairie grass
Are weaving in that clearing by the dam.
The creek's alive with crawfish and darters.
This spring the wild geraniums bloomed late
But lasted into May, almost to June.
The woods you memorized
                    rethink themselves.
The smallest movement of the brush will change
The portrait of a forest. That's mere art.
Your use of bark as snare and armature
To catch an anxious mind and hold it fast
Is more than artifice can do.
                      To know
The trails at night or drifted deep with snow,
To feel the roots beneath your shoes connect
To leaflets in the crowns of ash and oak,
To sense the Canadas before they swoop
Full-throated just above the canopy,
Is not to paint the woods,
                    but be them.
This copse at the crest of Hickory Hill
Draws trails, roads, and flyways together.
I come here for our conversations' sake,
Those models of reciprocal soundings,
Forgetting I can tell you nothing new
Now you're at one with everything in view.
You've become the elder and I keep still,
Attentive to each hint in these surroundings.

Alan Brody

Lessons from Pigg Farm

Keynote remarks
CIVIC Welcome Dinner for International Writers
Sept. 5, 2007

A year ago I retired from UNICEF and moved to Iowa City. Interaction with international writers was one of the attractions of Iowa, and I am honored to welcome that group tonight.

My wife Mary and I attended the final public reading by last year's international writers. We especially enjoyed a German writer's musings on the size and audacity of Iowa's squirrels, probably because one had just invaded our own house. Demonstrating that he had absorbed the American martial spirit, that writer summed up his findings with the observation that "an Iowa squirrel could kick a German squirrel's ass."

Others at that reading commented on Iowa City's remarkable experiment in conformism, where an entire community, completely free to express and dress itself in any way it pleases, elects to wear uniform colors of gold and black, with the letters I-O-W-A emblazoned across the chest. Two writers presented a duet on this subject. In apparent non-conformity they wore T-shirts with the letters A-W-O-I. On reflection, in a mirror that is, they were with us.

I believe there were also some observations on the American love affair with large cars and large houses. That was still advanced thinking a year ago, before the penguins in the movie "Happy Feet" caught President George W. Bush's attention and won a place for global warming in his State of the Union address.

We human beings seem to have a remarkable capacity for wishful thinking, whether it is about climate change, AIDS, or global terror. It seems to be our nature to fight against giving up present pleasures and prejudices, whether of sexual freedoms, freedom to drive a big car, or the certainty that God is on our side.

Who is to stand up to the power of such global wishful thinking? Some of last year's writers took on such questions in debates about the roles and responsibilities of the writer, as artist or as social and political activist.

America last September was in the midst of a national debate over torture. After all the sound and fury, our Congress caved in to authorize unprecedented violations of privacy and human rights. In the face of such bad politics, I could sense the activist writers were struggling over how to deal with emerging good feelings toward Iowa City. Sunsets over the Iowa River don't fit easily into black and white views of the world.

Perhaps some of this year's writers have friends back home who put similar pressure on you, demanding "Why in hell are you going to America?!" They will be watching you suspiciously on your return, for signs that you've become soft on Cheeseburger Culture.

Feelings of the world toward America seem to move in cycles. Many fell in love with John F. Kennedy, and then shared the disillusionment of America's own youth with racism, assassinations, and an ill-considered war in Vietnam. I was of that generation, joining the Peace Corps in 1968, and going into exile in Ghana for nearly ten years before I came to Iowa as a graduate student in 1978.

With the Watergate revelations of corruption and abuse of power, many in the 1970s thought America was in irreversible decline. Yet 20 years later, with the Cold War ended, its economy booming, its brands and commercial culture spreading across the globe, America appeared once again in ascension.

Now the cycle has turned again. And here we are in Iowa City, this autumn of 2007, in the midst of very interesting times. Candidates to be the next president of the United States seem to be on every street corner, fighting to win the hearts and minds of potential voters in the Iowa caucuses.

When you are not being distracted by Mrs. Clinton, Mr. Romney, Mr. Obama, and Mr. Giuliani arguing over who gets to sit with you at the breakfast table, you will in the coming months enjoy the privilege to be with each other — 35 writers from 31 countries here for the International Writers' Workshop's 40th anniversary year. What an opportunity!

I myself retired from my United Nations employment to pursue gray-haired aspirations of walking in the footsteps of Don Miguel de Cervantes. I have nominated myself for the "Don Quixote" award in recognition of my unstinting efforts, during 22 years in the U.N., to write clear prose.

Now an aspiring writer speaking to writers should tell his story with a story.

During my years in Ghana, I became interested in "Ananse Tales." These fables star the deeply-flawed Ananse the Spider and his clever son Ntikuma, who later resurfaced in African-American folklore as "Brer Rabbit" and his friends in the Uncle Remus tales.

In each of the places I later worked, I sought out that country's folk literature, for insights into the values and psychology of the people. In Turkey I made the acquaintance of Nasruddin Hodja and his donkey. In Afghanistan, I read a wonderful book of love stories, where I learned that when you cover every part of a woman's anatomy in a black burkha, it takes only the slightest flash of white flesh of a woman's neck or ankle to inflame a young man's passion, and drive him to destruction. In China, I learned that foxes can take on human form and become agents to repay injustice with stern justice.

When I became UNICEF's Representative in Swaziland, I discovered that fables like Ghana's Ananse tales were also a part of southern African traditional culture, and I began to write stories for use in "life skills education" programs. We reproduced some for church Sunday school classes. Focus groups told us they were loved by children and teachers alike. Swaziland's Ministry of Education became interested, and a South African publisher started work to prepare them for a wider publication.

Then my bureaucracy struck. In Johannesburg, the supply officer said, "Hold on! This is a printing job! Supply Division decides who does it!" When my memo of appeal reached our Supply Division in Denmark, someone there said, "Hold on! The legal officer in New York will have to look into this." The legal officer, two months later, said, "Hold on! Since when are Country Representatives supposed to write books? The Human Resources Director will have to look at this!" And the Human Resources Director wrote, "No staff member may publish a work without prior written permission from me. I am requesting your Regional Director to investigate this!"

As head of UNICEF's office in Swaziland, I was proud of making things happen on a scale of days and weeks. But these processes now dragged on over the months, in the midst of the world's worst HIV and AIDS epidemic, while Swaziland's teachers were asking, "Where are our life skills books?"

Of course, it was my own fault. Everyone was just doing their job, and I'm the one who made a habit of pushing the bureaucratic limits. Still, it was frustrating, and I woke up one night seething with anger, and yet laughing over an idea for a cartoon. In it, little Ms. Sisi Rabbit and her brother Bhuti, two characters from my fables, were locked up behind the bars of a jail cell. Standing in front of the cell, keys dangling from their belts, were two pigs serving as their jailers. One standing before a high stack of thick law books looked over the half-frames of his magnifying glasses at a book titled "Brother Lucky Dog's Lottery Pot of Money." The other pig standing in front of a stack of thick human resources manuals studied a small book entitled "The Forbidden Fru Fru Fruits Epidemic."

It occurred to me in my half sleep that, though I can't draw, a good writer ought to be able to produce this little satire as a fable. On the other hand, I thought, it might be, shall we say, impolitic to caricature the Director of Human Resources of one's organization as a pig.

As often happens with such things, the story I wrote that night turned out to be about something else. Its title is "The Road to Pigg Farm" (with apologies to George Orwell), and its lessons are the subject of my remarks tonight.

Once upon a time, when animals could talk and ran the world, a pig named Napoleon seized all the land from his neighbors, as far as the eye could see. He posted signs that said:

Pigg Farm Unltd.
Keep Out!

He spelled his surname "P-I-G-G." The double "g" was to ensure no one should mistake him for just any ordinary pig.

Napoleon Pigg's house had flush toilets with a special servant who filled the tank with water and pulled the chain. Everyone in his family were required to take three baths every day so no one would know how they smelled.

Pigg Farms grew corn and soybeans to feed millions of chickens that they kept in cages, under the watchful eyes of an army of weasels recruited from around the world. Every day the weasels took away the eggs and shipped them off as breakfast for someone else's table. "They are for export," Napoleon would say to any chicken that complained. "It's a global economy, you know."

A few eggs did go into incubators for hatching. Any chickens who complained or who became too old to produce their egg a day quota would be replaced by newly hatched young ones. The old and the complainers were not wasted, either. Their feathers were made into pillows, and their meat was ground up to make Pigg Farm Breakfast Sausage. Can you picture the advertisements? They said, "Chicken meat is good for the heart!"

Old Napoleon lived together with Mrs. Pigg and his two sons, Porker and Weenie Pigg, in a big mansion on the hill.

On the road up the hill to Pigg Farm, there was a constant movement of horses, donkeys, oxen, camels and llamas. They brought lace dresses and ostrich skin handbags for Mrs. Pigg, who was a fashion plate. They carried away eggs, feather pillows, and sausage to stock the supermarkets of the whole animal world.

Legions of sheep worked at very cheap wages to carry heavy buckets of water up the hill from the river. With the technology of the day, Napoleon Pigg could have easily pumped water to his house through pipes. "But why bother," he used to tell his friends over cigars, "when there are so many sheep to do it?"

Porker and Weenie Pigg liked to ride on large horses, whipping them to gallop up and down the road. "Hurry up!" they would shout to the other animals. "God hates a sluggard!"

One day, Porker and Weenie had dismounted from their horses and were resting by the roadside. By accident, Porker's eyes looked down toward the ground. "Look there, brother," he said. "I've never seen one of those before."

The humble creature he was observing was a Dung Beetle. The Dung Beetle family collected all the manure droppings that animals left on the road, fashioning them into round balls.

"Hey you, Insect!" Porker Pigg called out to the Dung Beetle. The Beetle's name was actually Daniel, and he was known among his own people as "Prince Daniel." He had never been called "Insect" before, so he didn't even look up from his work.

"That Insect is disrespectful," Weenie Pigg said to his brother. With his calfskin boot he kicked away the large ball of dung that "Prince Daniel" was laboriously pushing, and laughed as it rolled down the hill toward the river. Only then did the beetle look up to see who had disturbed his work.

"My brother is talking to you," Weenie Pigg sneered. "What do you think you're doing with that dung?"

"I am a Dung Beetle," Prince Daniel answered. "I make the dung into balls. I roll the balls from the road here, into the fields over there. I and my family use it to roof our house, and to cook, and to fertilize the flowers. The bees make honey from the flowers, and they share that with the orphaned crickets whose mothers and fathers were squashed on the road."

"The road to Pigg Farm belongs to the Piggs," Porker Pigg interrupted him. "Everything on it belongs to us. Do you have a letter of permission from our father to collect dung from our road?"

"I didn't know I needed a letter," Prince Daniel replied. "It's in our Dung Beetle nature to collect dung wherever we find it, and to make something beautiful from it. Even this ball you just kicked away, you see how far it rolled, that's because of my good craftsmanship. You think it's just dung, but there is beauty in that, too..."

"Shut up!" Porker Pigg interrupted him. "Dung also has commercial value! If we catch you trying to steal it again, we will crush you!"

"So be it," Prince Daniel answered. And without another word he disappeared into the field.

"I guess we showed him," Weenie Pigg said, grunting with laughter, and his brother Porker joined in. No one had ever before heard that kind of grunting sound, though it has become the common speech of pigs ever since.

After Prince Daniel the Dung Beetle disappeared into the field, taking his family and people with him, the animal droppings began to pile up on the road. Soon it was so thick that the animals slipped in it. When it rained, the manure washed into the river and polluted it. The polluted water made the chickens sick, and they all died. The fields where corn and soybeans grew missed the manure, and crops became stunted. Angry about the reduced rations, the cows broke down their barn door and fled.

The pigs ran out to chase the cows. But the mighty horses that the Piggs used to ride had become lame from infections in their hooves, forcing the pigs to walk just like all the other animals. Slipping and sliding in the manure, they couldn't catch up, and the cows got away forever.

When the pigs got home their bodies were covered with filth. They got into their bathtubs to wash it off, but without enough water, it was nothing but a stinking mud bath. That's why, to this day, a place where pigs bathe is no longer called a bathtub, but a "pigsty."

Napoleon Pigg made inquiries to understand what had gone wrong on his estates. Old Watchdog told him about the disappearance of Prince Daniel, and Napoleon went to search for him.

Napoleon didn't even know what a Dung Beetle looked like. Eventually, he found a simple field beetle in the weed-patch that used to be his soybean farm.

"Mr. Dung Beetle!" he addressed him. "Prince of Insects! I am ruined! Please come back to my road and do your job again!"

"What job is that, Mr. Pigg?" the field beetle asked.

"To collect the dung, of course, and make something useful of it," Napoleon replied.

"Oh, that's Prince Daniel you're looking for," the other said. "They tell me he's retired and gone away forever. I'm a simple field beetle. It's not just anyone that can make something special out of ordinary shit on the road."

And that's how pigs ceased to be rulers and became what they are today.

So when you see someone eating bacon with their eggs, or tucking into a big pork barbecue sandwich, I hope you will remember my story and the lessons of the rude and greedy brothers Pigg.

As I sat down to write this story two years ago, I didn't want to give those I was going to caricature as pigs any grounds to charge me with insubordination. That was the genesis of the Dung Beetle as hero. If I portrayed myself as such a humble creature, I thought, anyone who complained my story had insulted him would just be laughed at.

As I'm sure many of the writers here know, stories often become something more than the incidents that provoked them. The Road to Pigg Farm, once started, took its own course, and in my view became a fable about the unappreciated role of the artist in society.

So many serious writers struggle for survival in materialistic societies where "worth" is measured only by wealth. They write and try to make something of beauty and value out of the mess of life in their deeply flawed environments. I suspect many of you here tonight labor thus, like Prince Daniel on the road to Pigg Farm.

However, I suspect tonight is the first time — and no doubt you hope it is the last — that anyone compliments you by comparing you to a Dung Beetle.

Tonight we of Iowa City salute you, our esteemed visitors for Iowa's 2007 International Writers' Workshop. It is an honor and a privilege to have you with us.

You have come to a special place. In terms of respect for those who dedicate themselves to the written word, I know no place in the world quite like this little "city state." In the moral order of Iowa City, the writer is royalty. And the Iowa citizens and taxpayers who support the University of Iowa's writing programs are the humble laborers who help to create this supportive community for writers.

In Iowa City, the Prince Daniels of our fable tonight are thus not only the writers present, but also the unsung citizens of our host organization, CIVIC, who labor as volunteers to smooth the road that will be traveled by international visitors. I salute all of you volunteers here tonight, who represent America's best traditions of openness and hospitality.

The story-tellers in Ghana, at the end of every tale, traditionally finish with these words: "This my story which I have told, if it be sweet, or if it be not sweet, take some elsewhere, and let some come back to me." Thank you.

Mary Vermillion

Teaching English in War Time

A farm boy who claims to hate
reading deep leaves for the Gulf.
Every morning I offer more King Lear
to those who remain. We think we know
storms and fools and mistakes
that cannot be fixed.

Then towers fall.
An Army girl leaps and pirouettes
through Chaucer, but withdraws from the Bard
and misses Milton's Satan, Shelley's lark,
years of beauty while she prepares for war.
My grade book swells with zeros.

A year passes. She returns from Baghdad,
garrisoned in silence. Her classmates
pillage Gulliver's Travels and blithely
critique evils of war they have not seen.

I return from summer to Shakespeare,
new faces and old questions: Is Branagh's
"Henry Five" anti-war? We cannot decide.
A lieutenant, a slender tardy girl
who loves the Guard and wins easy As,
plays Lady Macbeth: Unsex me here.
Here, you spirits. Here.

After Iraq
she watches the same movie every night.
Every night she summons the same flat screen,
seeking a place where she can always know
exactly what will happen next, a land
with a clear beginning, middle, and end.

L. Ward McFarlane

The Van Pool's Grace

■ ■ ■

Grace smiled to herself, her head leaning back against the van's headrest and her eyes closed to block out the bright early morning sunlight. Two of her van pool colleagues, Peggy and Loretta, were at it again. This time it was about Mrs. Miller from the town's grocery and what young Yonnie Mast was reported to have called her after he stole some candy from her store. The precise word, and exactly what it meant, had varied no less than four times in the 24 hours Grace had heard the story repeated around town. In a town of 437 souls the event was big news and bound to be discussed at least through next Thursday.

Peggy was now insisting on a fifth version.

"Well," said Peggy, drawing out the "el" sound, "I don't know what Mrs. Hirsch told you, or why she thinks she knows, because I heard it from Mrs. Miller's Sarah herself."

"Well," countered Loretta with saccharin sweetness, "all I know is Mrs. Hirsch said she was in the store at the very time it happened, buying flour and milk."

"Well, it's not what I heard," Peggy reiterated with equally counterfeit geniality. "And imagine, that such a child would say such a thing, it just shows you how the 1980s have changed so many of our families."

The air inside the van became heavier, almost palpable, like a drop in pressure before a thunderstorm, as Peggy and Loretta continued to dig at each other. Most people would never know there was tension by their words or the tone of their voices. They sounded like two ladies having a simple conversation, perhaps a slight disagreement over some minor details. But Grace knew the stakes; only one of them could earn the title of being right. She could just imagine how much they were both seething inside, hearts pounding, puffed up like two Tom turkeys about to fight. This time she had more trouble trying to hide her smile and had to raise her head a moment and pretend to cough. She opened her eyes briefly and saw that no one had noticed, including Peggy and Loretta. They were still busy mentally circling each other.

Now that her eyes were open Grace looked around from her center left seat. Peggy sat immediately to her right, indeed looking slightly swollen and indignant. Loretta was in the back seat, immediately behind Peggy. They weren't able to make eye contact so that permitted them to ratchet up the quarrel a little bit. From the corner of her right eye she could just make out Dan Fisher sitting in the middle of the back seat, reading a newspaper and trying to appear as if he heard nothing going on around him. Alice Dunne was directly behind Grace, out of her line of sight, but Grace could imagine her counting crochet stitches; she thought she was working on another baby blanket for a cousin's new grandchild.

Grace turned to face forward again, her eyes resting against the frizzy auburn curls of Nan Jessup, the van's driver. Nan was engaged in a lively discussion with her habitual shotgun seat companion, Christy Black. Nan and Christy both had positions in middle administration at the hospital so knew each other fairly well, had lunch together frequently, went jogging together back home, and sometimes had each other's young families over for dinner. Grace knew this because she had overheard them mention these things through the years. They didn't often converse with her directly, although they were unfailingly polite when they did.

The van seats were not assigned. Well, actually, yes and no. A few years ago when the van pool was new the van members had taken a vote, orchestrated by Christy, that it would be easiest for everyone to keep the same seats, and that consideration should be given based on the order they were dropped off each morning. Grace was assigned the front passenger seat. This had lasted a few weeks until Nan and Christy became good friends, then Christy unceremoniously began taking the front passenger seat. Everyone from then on kept the same seating arrangement. Grace would no sooner think of retaking the front, or taking Loretta's back seat spot, than she would take someone else's sandwich from the fridge at the office. It was someone else's marked territory, you just didn't cross those lines. It would be the same for all of them; where they came from personal space and belongings had very definite boundaries. Except Christy, but then she'd only lived there for about ten years or so.

Grace turned her attention to the scenery, fields of knee-high corn and stands of trees zooming by, streaks of a hundred shades of green. Grace was always glad of her seat because she was on the opposite side of the rising and setting sun, so didn't have to deal with the bright glare and direct heat like Peggy and Loretta did. It didn't bother Christy to be on the right side of the van because she sat directly in front of the air conditioning vents and would often turn them to blow on her directly as she chatted with Nan. Grace would watch her do this in the middle of a conversation, as if Christy was unconscious of her own actions. Grace knew Christy was faking it every time and was fully aware that doing so would keep the cool air from spreading to the back of the van. Grace also knew the others noticed this as well, certainly Peggy and Loretta would discuss it when they left the van each night. But just like taking each other's seats it would be rare for someone to comment directly on Christy's selfishness. It should have been obvious.

Sooner than she expected the van pulled onto the exit ramp and headed into the big town. They headed to the east side of the river where Grace, Peggy, and Loretta would be dropped off near the main part of campus before the others headed back to the hospital side.

Peggy and Loretta filed out of the van and began walking toward their offices at the center of campus. "You both have a good day," called Grace good naturedly as she exited the van.

"Oh, Grace, thanks, you too," called Peggy. Loretta waved and resumed their conversation. Grace was a very nice lady, but she never gossiped — not that Peggy and Loretta would ever refer to it as gossip — so she tended to be overlooked at times.

Grace took the elevator up to her office on the fifth floor of the small campus building. The hallway lights were still off, all the office doors down the hall closed save one at the end. That would be Professor Kim, who always came in to work around 5:30 every morning. Professor Kim seemed to take the "publish or perish" dictum to heart, but Grace knew she was just a very prolific producer. Grace often heard the faculty speculating in the break room across from her office that Professor Kim would probably retire soon. She would be sorry to lose the welcoming light at the end of the hallway, particularly on winter mornings when it was still dark outside and the fifth floor cold and full of shadows.

As she turned right she reached out to flip the light switches. Since it was the middle of summer, few of the faculty would be coming in. She expected her own boss to show up in a couple hours and stay until after lunch. This didn't concern Grace; she had worked in the department for 23 years and was quite capable of handling any problem thrown her way by the students, faculty, other offices, even the occasional parent.

The exception was a phone call from the Dean. Always the Dean wanted to speak to the Chair immediately and without fail the Chair was impossible to find. Grace had long ago given up wondering how some Chairs would spend a few hours a day or even per week in the job while others would put in 10-hour days, and no one seemed to notice the difference. But when the Dean called it was always urgent and Grace knew she was to understand it was her own shortcoming if she didn't always know the whereabouts of her own Chair. Such was the case this morning; her Chair arrived around 11:30, annoyed that she had missed another important call from the Dean.

"Grace, I don't know why you couldn't have called me at home. I was working there all morning and you could have easily phoned to tell me the Dean needed me," she chided. "Imagine how that makes me look. I do wish you would think of things like that sometimes."

Grace's eyes slid briefly to the shopping bag her Chair was holding. "Oh, I am sorry, Margaret," Grace said serenely, not mentioning that she had phoned the Chair at home every 20 minutes for the last three hours.

"Alright, no harm done, I suppose," said the Chair. "I had better go call the Dean." She smiled brightly at Grace and went to her own office.

Grace viewed the approaching lunch hour with some secret displeasure. The Chair was taking her out to lunch today. She would have preferred to visit the library, but it was time for the obligatory quarterly lunch.

It wasn't so bad. As usual Grace sat quietly but attentively as her boss talked of the many places she had recently visited, the people she met, what her husband and children were doing over the summer. This meant her boss was habitually slow to finish her own lunch while Grace would finish well in advance, so she had learned to pace herself. Otherwise, if Grace finished her food too early, her boss would sometimes remember that polite conversation was often two-sided and would ask her questions about herself. She might ask about special projects in the office or how the student assistant was working out, which was OK. Sometimes she would ask about living in such a small town, adding comments along the way that would be generally insulting to any Iowan. It used to surprise Grace to hear the extreme stereotypes regarding small-town life, the jokes about accents or linguistic practices.

Worst of all, particularly if the Chair chose to have a glass or two of wine, she would lean toward Grace in an ill-suited conspiratorial way and attempt to query

Grace about her "love life." Grace could adroitly deflect such inquiries, but she resented having to do so and felt slightly embarrassed for her boss, who should know the boundaries well enough.

Her boss never heard details about her volunteer work, or about the depressed elderly mother who lived with Grace, or the books and television programs Grace enjoyed. She'd never be told about the young daughter Grace lost all those years ago, or the relief work she had done in Korea after the war. Even if her boss or others had ever thought to ask, those were private personal things that Grace would not share with strangers. Fortunately today her boss was in a hurry so lunch passed quickly.

An hour later Grace's Work-Study assistant, Stephanie, arrived at work. Grace was so efficient and capable she really had no need for an assistant, but each year she asked her Chair to apply for Work-Study funding and each year received enough to have a student come in for fifteen hours each week. The students were always interesting, although they varied widely in terms of competency. Still, they could use the money and Grace made a point of having sufficient funding to keep them employed; she knew every little bit helped.

This was Stephanie's second year with the office. As student assistants went she was fairly competent and handled the various small tasks Grace assigned her uncomplainingly. Grace was entertained by her conversation and her accounts of various weekend escapades or trips with friends. Sometimes they would meet for lunch. Stephanie never noticed that Grace seldom shared stories about her own life; she took it for granted that there weren't any.

Grace was particularly entertained by watching Stephanie's ongoing flirtations with one of the graduate students while simultaneously making eyes at one of the very married associate professors. Of course Grace had seen it before, far too many times. Her placement in the hall permitted her a wide view of the commons area and the acoustics on the floor carried plenty of conversations her way. And she had heard many conversations over the years. She remembered her student assistant Steve back in '78, and the young visiting instructor. The visiting instructor's contract had not been renewed the following year.

In Stephanie's case Grace couldn't decide if something would ultimately transpire with the graduate student or with the faculty member. Grace decided to put her money on the faculty member. If she ended up choosing correctly, she'd reward herself with that new handbag she had her eye on. She'd need something cheerful to make up for the unavoidable emotional mess that would soon after explode around the department. It was very unfortunate, but so predictable. Still, Grace would never be the source for spreading rumors and innuendos; what Grace saw or heard stayed with Grace.

Mid-afternoon the new assistant professor came in. This fall would be his first semester, so he was organizing his office and files. He was a quiet, pleasant young man and seemed to adopt Grace as a motherly confidant. He had even shyly invited her to lunch last week. She knew people often viewed her as safe and sanguine. She also knew that this would gradually change over the years, say, in about three. As he lost that sense of being new and not fully belonging to the department, the ubiquitous social stratum that separated faculty from support staff would widen. By degrees over the next few years he would grow increasingly distant. He'd of course remain very friendly, stopping by occasionally to chat and have a laugh. But it would be different. Of course not all faculty followed this trend, like Professor Kim. But most did. The social division was just the way things were. There was no point in being filled with indignation or hurt as so many other secretaries were. Grace would not expect to be invited to a dinner party.

The rest of the afternoon was peaceful and uneventful, and at 4:45 p.m. Grace stood waiting at the corner to catch the van pool.

The atmosphere on the ride home was more subdued. She noted Christy leaning back in her seat, eyes closed, not speaking to Nan. She wondered if there had been some breach between the two of them and thought perhaps Nan had learned about and not appreciated the jog Christy had taken with Nan's husband Saturday afternoon while Nan was out of town at a conference. Grace had seen them pass by on the gravel road behind her house. But then she observed both women seemed relaxed and comfortable, so put it down to end-of-day weariness. Dan and Alice chatted quietly and companionably as Alice crocheted. Peggy and Loretta were now comradely allies, with Loretta spouting how one of her faculty had tried to get her to type up some personal letters, in triplicate no less, and Peggy offering sympathetic exclamations. Grace herself leaned back and closed her eyes. It was nice to relax.

She enjoyed the short walk home from the van drop-off as always, waving across the street to Mrs. Miller, who stood sweeping the sidewalk in front of her grocery store. As she passed the drug store she considered stopping in for a vanilla Coke but decided today she was just a little too weary, and needed to head home to make supper for Mother.

Grace stepped onto the sidewalk leading to the front door of her small house, but circled to the back yard to her lush vegetable garden. She picked a small yellow squash and pulled some carrots for their supper.

As Grace entered through the back door, her mother looked up.

"What could you be doing coming in that way?" she wondered out loud. "You're awfully late tonight. You know my stomach is sensitive and can't take eating late or I'll be up all night with the reflux." She then went back to staring glumly at her television program. Grace, on time as usual, said nothing but kissed her mother's forehead in greeting and cheerfully set about fixing supper.

She sautéed the small squash and boiled the carrots well so they would be soft enough for her mother to eat; she had stopped wearing her dentures years ago. She opened a can of tomato soup and fixed a grilled cheese sandwich, cutting it in half diagonally to share between them. After setting the table she called her mother into the kitchen to eat. They sat down at the green Formica table.

Her mother frowned slightly at the fare. "Lots of yellow and orange tonight," she said querulously. "Hope the carrots are cooked." She slurped her soup as the kitchen clock ticked.

Grace watched her mother for a moment until she was satisfied that tonight she would dine fairly cooperatively. Her mother looked up at her between slurps, an annoyed expression on her face. "You always look like the cat that ate the canary, like you know everything." She went back to slurping.

Grace thought about all the knowledge she'd accumulated over the years, about her coworkers, neighbors, van pool colleagues. Never once had she shared any of it with anyone, but some days she dreamed, what if she was to begin? "I do know everything, don't I, Mother," she agreed, then smiled her beatific smile and began to eat.

Tamara Batie

The Map

■ ■ ■

You hear the native bells, see the tribal markings in my face, trace the map of my ancestors, when you carress my breasts, the hills and plains of my naval and hips, the well of life that springs from between my thighs, the truth of struggle and toil lie behind these eyes and happiness reigns in the form of a smile, I am the child of before, the caretaker of now and the mother of the future, every cell of my being has a story to tell, weaving tales of african rituals, the middle passage, and why I'm allergic to cotton, from the badseeds to the "Oh, no child i can't do that, you know i'm saved," It's in the swish of my hips when I step forward or gravitate back, In the hand on my hip, eyes rollin, head shakin, pop of my lips, It's in the open door policy, the come and eat your fill then lie your head on my couch, because we are his least, lest be none less to you, seeing my GOD in the face of my children, your children, because any child in my life is mine, Feel the wariness of my feet for I have traveled many lands, loving each of you so that you might give love too, Do Not forget the past while not looking back, because if you forget them, have you ever known me, I am the child of before, the caretaker of now, and the mother of the future, come sit at my feet and suckle on my words as I explain to you the map of our ancestors.

Andy Douglas

The Best Things Happen Slowly

■ ■ ■

Rain seeps from the sky. Lounging in bed, under the weather, I'm in need of some redemption. Saxophonist Archie Shepp's breathy life force pours through brass and reed. Goin' Home. Htttt htttt, his teased-out trills and staccato stops wash over my body, the steam rising slowly around me, curling, wreathing, pulling my head under the comforting water, stealing my breath away.

The rain seeps down. And I'm floating on my back, lazily drifting in circles, borne by the steadfast current, down to where the Rivers Jordan and Mississippi collide.

There's a bittersweetness in these lines. You can hear Shepp longing to dip his instrument deeper into the inky well of being, to come up with an infinitude of variations. And you can hear the sadness of American history.

The pianist kindly offers a pullout pallet upon which the sax player may lay his tired bones down. He's tired; he's been wandering in the desert, for years. And here, like a sponge to his lips, the suddenly emphatic, now softly yielding, melody, to guide him on his way.

Horace Parlin is the rhythm section of one. No femur-rattling stride bounce here. But something about the spare, pared-down sound moves me. An elegant sadness. It's self-contained. It bears the absence of any other percussive support.

The hues of pianist Parlin's palette are in all the changes. The color of autumn leaves. Smoke. Bright Sunday dresses. Gospel roots wind 'round these riffs like wisteria. And there, there in Shepp's response to Parlin's call is a whiff of Coltrane. Fluttering up the scale, not taking the stairs one at a time, but shimmying up the banister, scaling the drainpipe.

Now pianist and saxophonist, two old friends, take a little road trip in a big black Buick down by the levee. And me in the back seat. The land rolls by, endless telephone poles with surging wires, twilight diners, white clapboard churches, fields of wheat and alfalfa. Always moving on. But always — restrained. Cruising on a two-lane highway, cars start to pile up behind us, trying to force us to pick up the speed. We keep it at 35.

There's a longing that underlies these riffs, an evolutionary imperative. Desire, but restrained desire. A willingness to let silence do what it was created to do. The best things happen slowly.

Shepp keeps the rhythm loose. He keeps the rhythm sliding and slow. Time is pulled out like taffy, its billowing substance stretched to breaking point. Then Shepp slips in again through the rift and inhabits it wholly.

Syncopation, it's called, a simple, steady pulse disrupted by a delayed accent. Syncope is also the medical term for dizziness, a temporary suspension of breath, of circulation. We swoon. The blood takes a little break, the breath goes on holiday, pulled under the water, for … just … a … moment longer. Then, it's there again, back where it should be. But everything is different, bathed in new light.

The sax says, take a script. Play it. Act it out. Again. Set the stage. Then do the unexpected thing.

And do it slowly.

John Birkbeck

Geography Song

I held your place
in line in front of
The Coffee Jag place
on half price night
and they were gonna play
those jumpy riffs
just for you
on the snare drums
and you said you
were just going out
for cigarettes and
just as that sank in
I got a postcard from you
with palm trees
and big gaudy red stamps
and a weird alphabet —
you always do that to me
but at least you always
come back and take
your place in line.

Jeff Charis-Carlson

Small World

■ ■ ■

"Are you sure I can't do anything?" James sits awkwardly on the wooden kitchen stool. Dishes from the earlier tea party fill the small breakfast table and the countertops. Clotheslines and towel-lines shoot from a nail on the far wall to spiderweb eighteen inches below the ceiling.

"No, just sit there. Don't worry. I can handle it." Natasha answers while leaving the kitchen to get some eggs and butter from the hallway refrigerator. Somehow decades of feminism have ingrained too deeply into his psyche. He can't sit idly by while she prepares all this food. How chauvinistic! How anachronistic! How insulting?! Yet, he is the American, and she is the Russian. Perhaps women's liberation hasn't reached Russia yet. Should he enlighten her? He should do something more than just sit there.

When she returns, he states, "There must be something I can do!?"

She just smiles, takes out a bowl, begins cracking the eggs and says, "No. Just sit there."

James decides to do just that. He moves his stool toward the counter area and begins to clear enough dishes away to lean on his arm. Crack, Bang, and "Oops!" are heard simultaneously as his newly moved dishes begin to fall.

"You can not try to break all my dishes," Natasha says sarcastically and triumphantly. She smiles.

Her smile gazes deep. The allure of her jet black hair mixes with the shine from her teeth. Both effects collide around the center of her rounded face — at her slightly pointed nose. The colors of her green-mustard-red-black quarter-checkered shirt clash with her purple glasses, but the contrast, rather than breaking any fashion rule, highlights her smile. And, as if focused by her glasses, the power of that smile, and the power of that gaze, makes James realize that she knows exactly what she is doing. She consciously chooses for him not to help.

He remembers trying to stir the sugar only to have her say, "I just put white sugar on the top so no one would see the brown. Now look what you've done." Or the time, no matter where he sat, he was always sitting in her way. Now, he can't even stack dishes without causing a ruckus.

"Well, I'll listen to you this time. I'd hate to touch something I wasn't supposed to and have you yell at me, again," he says while leaning forward so she can open the silverware drawer.

"When have I yelled at you?" she asks with a knife in hand.

"Every time I try to do something helpful."

She just smiles and begins to cut the sausage.

James lets it all sink in. The potato peels in the sink mean that she has taken the time to peel six potatoes. The dirty dishes scattered around mean that she will have to spend much time cleaning up after he leaves — he tried to help her clean last night, but she wouldn't allow it. A few flies crawl on the overhead web-like clotheslines as sausage sizzles in the frying pan.

Fried sausage! In all his six weeks in St. Petersburg he's had nothing but raw sausage with bread and cheese (the staple of the Russian diet). Imagine having fried sausage with a meal. It's more than he could have thought to ask.

"Do you want your eggs just fried or, I think the work is 'omelette,' fried with milk?" She asks staring over the frying pan.

After he answers, "Just fried will do fine," she pours the eggs over the sausage.

"How ingenious," James thinks to himself. Again more than he could have hoped. Fried eggs with the sausage — a real, cared-over, home-cooked meal. Not the impersonal hotel food that he's used to. Natasha offered to cook all this just to be nice; just to make him feel special; just to make him feel at home. But, he isn't exactly at home. He can't help without being yelled at. He doesn't understand all the cultural rules — like why you have to take your shoes off when eating in a Russian's house — but he feels at ease.

Natasha has been different. She's Russian but speaks beautiful English. If she doesn't know the right word, she performs a verbal dance around the concept — creating poetry out of simple expressions: "walking" becomes "traveling by foot," "glasses" reverts into "spectacles," and "I'm ticklish" becomes "I have great fear over being touched like that."

In her library scores of Russian books shout their Russian characters. James only sounds out the alphabet; he doesn't know all the meanings. He feels comfortable reading the Cyrillic letters for "Tolstoy," and "Dostoevsky," and "Puskin." But, there in the hodgepodge of unreadable writings is an English copy of "The Great Gatsby." A familiar book amid the strange. He doesn't understand it all, but he still enjoys it.

Natasha continues to stand over the stove. As the potatoes boil on the front right burner, she mans the frying pan on the front left. Steam rises from the food and circles around her. James watches the swirls as they dance. Her push-parted hair begins to fall because of the heat. Pushing it back into place, she transforms her face into an expression of regal power. Her actions are controlled. She has considered all their consequences. With her head cocked and her mouth half smiling, she slyly says, "Why are you smiling?"

James didn't notice he had been smiling. But, he isn't shocked by the news. Before he realizes, he says the words, "Because I'm looking at you." At that moment, the phrase becomes a game between them. The flow of words proves natural, even usual, and James envisions saying the words back and forth many times in the future — just like the way she would address him as "Sir ..." and he would respond " ... Ma'am."

Originally, she had thought that these were everyday sayings. Learners of a new language usually over-formalize all conversations. The assumed importance of formality made him feel important. Just as the time, effort, and sacrifice of preparing a meal makes him feel important — at least, important to her. His thoughts of enlightening her to modern ways were insulting. This is a modern Russian, independent woman, who is offering him the gift of feeling special. With all involved in this meal, how can he help but smile when he looks at her.

The sound of the words "Because I'm looking at you" begin to die down. With their dying is an elongated period of silence. Not an awkward time, but almost a dramatic pause before Natasha turns toward the frying pan and casually says, "I like it when you look at me."

This response completely surprises James. His imagined game had played out to its pre-imagined form. She grows accustomed to his gaze. He likes to look at her.

He enjoyed catching her eye during boring meetings or during work time. But now, with no other social demands, he truly enjoys looking at her.

Natasha begins to spatula the sides of the eggs from the pan. James watches her go all the way around the pan before asking, "What do you mean, you 'like it' when I look at you?" He intensifies his gaze.

"I mean most people make me feel uncomfortable when they look at me. You don't. I like it ... understand?"

James simply says, "Da ... Yes," while Natasha turns off the potatoes and dishes the eggs onto plates.

"Can you take the potatoes and the rack out to the table?" she asks.

"Da."

"Thank you ... Sir."

Happy to finally help, James says, "You're welcome ... Ma'am," and goes to the table — anxious to eat.

Nick Smith

Iowa

I saw her this morning: a bright flash
of light behind the mulberry tree,
in half-shadow. The smell of corn is
with me — a sharp smell stronger than
the mulberries, and softly I heard her
voice as if it came from the tree, a voice
of clear, faint memories.

She is like dawn, standing alone
against the day. Her eyes look to far
off places, beckoning. I am surprised
by her face — young and old together.
She does not speak directly but murmurs
from the tree or the corn. She stands and
looks — looks at me — strong and frail
like a statue. I've made her from all
that ever happened, and I cannot
catch her.

Adele Bonney
Horseback Writer

some days
I mount lightly
my seat locks gently to your back
my legs form around your willing flanks
their slightest pressure sends your haunches
down, tightening, pressing
I feel your muscle and my will
converge as we step and step each word
with smooth, deliberate motion

striding out
we whisper up and down the reins
channeling our power into
flowing, bending curves
I rise and sit
in perfect time

and then we sail
over wide, grassy lakes, you changing
leads on the fly
in response to my slightest shift
of meaning
until we lose all our syllables
in a headlong surge

other days
my foot's barely
in the stirrup and
you shy, wild-eyed
I land heavily on you, a clumsy weight
your violent head bobbing
jerks the reins in my hands
we lurch ahead in
disjointed syntax

when I try to coerce a
smoother cadence you
trip
over nothing and
stagger upright, then
buck
I jump down and
stomp off.

Linda Bolton

The Painter, the Sculptor, the Poet

The painter, the sculptor, the poet:
these are the storytellers, the caretakers of culture,
the new makers of myth.
These are the worried hearts
in our midst, who usher us
towards remembrance
and the liberating power of imagination.
"We are who we imagine ourselves to be,"
my teacher taught me.
Then, I remembered:
It is the stories that hold us together,
whole the spirit and heal our broken souls.
Who we choose to become
will demand a refusal to forget, and
an act of the imagination, so powerful
that even history can begin anew.

Chris Kilgore

A Variation on a Theme IV

I good friend of mine, with whom I discuss literature and politics and so forth, met me out for drink not long ago. He'd brought along part of a manuscript that he was working on which contained the following story.

I'd always considered Luke my friend, even though the only bond between us was the writing of fiction. Our relationship had been established this way when we shared a creative writing class in college and although we became fast friends, taking an interest in each others' work, discussing what we loved and hated about literature and writing, the fact of the matter was that we had very little in common. Even in college our personalities were dissimilar; Luke was ambitious and driven, whereas I was always somewhat at a loss for what to make of myself. He was uncompromising in his beliefs and would defend them at all occasions, and at any cost, with incredible powers of oration. For my part, I was never sure whether I believed in everything or nothing at all, and I was, more often than not, the sounding board for everyone's ideas but my own. We never hung out together in a group and didn't have any friends in common, and after our undergrad he went on to grad school, got married, had a daughter, got a job as a professor and bought a house; all in the same time in which I lived in several cities in several states, working various jobs for little pay, dating a few different women, living paycheck to paycheck in a host of dilapidated one-bedroom apartments. Yet in spite of our contrasts the only person that either of us still spoke to from our college years was each other.

Writing may have been our only bond, but it was a powerful one and we were equally passionate for it. Over the years any time either of us had written something that was ready to be read — if a story seemed to be lacking something, if we couldn't quite get a character right, a dialog was unnatural or the pacing felt wrong — we knew that the other could be counted on as an honest and sincere critic. The value of that service to each other was enough to endure years, relocations, and all of the differences of our personalities and daily lives.

The story that Luke brought me to read that fall was typical of all of his fiction in both quality and style. It was almost perfectly written, consisting of paragraphs consisting of sentences, consisting of words that read as if not one of them could have been arranged in any other way. The content of the tale bore the characteristic stamp of his biting satire and was aimed, as was much of his fiction, at the hypocrisies of the religious. In this incarnation, the main characters were two intellectuals who fall into a rare kind of love, deep, natural and soulful. Of all of the beliefs they hold in common, the one that they feel most akin is their atheism, which they feel liberates them to love in a way that is more honest, more personal, and most importantly, stronger than if somehow God, in the form of fate, had brought them together, and so could tear them apart. Then at the place in the narrative where their feelings for each other have been confirmed and the reader feels inspired at the consummation of this modern fairy tale, tragedy strikes in the form of a car accident, which leaves the female character in a desperate state. In this time of need, the male character finds himself alone and, with no hope left, turns to God for salvation, to the same God of whose renunciation was the foundation for his love. His prayer is answered in the form of a flatline on the bedside EKG of the woman, leaving the man, in the end, bereft, not only of his love, but also of his dignity and possibly his entire personal identity. I got the impression that the story was a jab at some of Luke's peers, who were getting to the age when their mortality was beginning to loom ever larger and not having the same courage of their convictions that he does, typically began to reconsider their stance on religion.

He'd sent it to me in an e-mail a couple days before we were to meet and discuss it, at which time I told him how well I thought it was written. In addition I told him that I thought it was funny, poignant, and in the end, heartbreakingly sad.

"But what?" he wanted to know, aware that I was uncharacteristically withholding some criticism from him.

"Well," I told him, "It's just that it's kind of a bummer, you know?"

"A bummer?" his expression widened into a grin, "I suppose that's the point. You think it's overly sadistic?"

"It's just that your characters are so well constructed that by the end of the story I feel like I really know them, like they're my own friends. So naturally, at the end when he's destitute, asking for a miracle, I just wonder ... Why can't you grant it? It could work; in the end God does exist, and he comes through in the hour of need; sort of a Prodigal Son type of story. It could be inspirational."

"You're serious," he remarked, and at this, burst out laughing and kept it up for long enough to make me begin to feel uncomfortable, and somewhat put off. "That's not what the story's about." He said finally, and I could detect a little bit of hostility in the way his words came out. "I don't write inspirational stories. People that want to be inspired shouldn't read my work, they should read Chicken-Soup-for-the-Goddamned-Soul or some of that shit. The very point I'm trying to make with this story is that people who turn to 'God' when it's convenient for them are hypocrites.

'God' doesn't exist, which is obvious to any rational person, so just because you decided to believe in him doesn't suddenly cause him to exist."

"But God does exist," I countered, somewhat humbly, aware that I was facing down a merciless rhetorician. "Or at any rate, he exists for your characters. It's you."

The look in Luke's eyes softened a bit, and for a minute he said nothing, but just looked away wearing an amused expression, a grin tugging at the corners of his mouth. Then he said, "I'm not God. I'm just a writer. There is a difference."

"Is there?" I asked. "Who created these characters, who created every last detail about them, including all of the people around them, their surroundings, the world they live in, their universe? You are God, man. You have complete omnipotence. What if we were characters in a story. What if, right now in some other dimension some author is writing the story of us sitting here talking, saying these exact things? Wouldn't that author fit the description of what's commonly referred to as God?"

"I suppose, but there isn't someone writing us right now."

"How do you know that for a fact?"

"Because we're real, they're not. We were born and have lives, we don't just exist out of nowhere for a few pages and then disappear"

"Do they know they're not real? Do they know they don't have any pasts? Do they know they only exist for a few pages? Even though you didn't write it, don't your characters have a background that you could give them if you needed to? Couldn't you create millennia of past for your story in a few seconds? How do you know that it's not the same for us? How do you know that our pasts aren't just some construction? I mean can you live in your past? Can you touch it? It's just an idea, so how do you know that it's not the idea of some divine author?"

All of this led into a long discussion, between us, on God and writing, the divine aspects of the act of creation, and the responsibility, if any, of the creator to his creation. It was a fair dialog, Luke listened to my point of view attentively, and delivered his rebuttal with a cool head, and in the end he disagreed with everything I said. He conceded with a dismissive gesture of his hands that it was an interesting literary motif, but as a philosophy, which asserted that God actually was just a writer creating the universe for literary purposes, it was childish at best, closer to ridiculous, bordering on delusional. He told me this in a good natured way, of course, no offense intended. Nonetheless, I left offended, but before I did I finished my point.

"All I'm saying," I said, "is that you can answer the prayers of your character, you can make it so the girl lives in the end, you have that power. It might not be anything to you — it's just a story — but put yourself in the place of your character. He's asking you for a miracle, and you can grant it with just a few keystrokes. That much you can't deny. That's all I'm saying." Then I left, and it wasn't until I'd heard of the accident several months later that I saw or spoke to him again.

Luke's teenage daughter, a freshman in high school was out driving around the country roads with her friends, they'd been drinking and the driver ran a stop sign and got T-boned by full-sized pickup truck. She was in a coma, and the prognosis was not good. By the time I'd heard about it and was able to get a hold of him, the doctors were pretty sure that she was not going to make it. They said it would be a miracle if she ever regained consciousness. I went to the hospital to see him and do what I could, which I expected would be nothing. What can you do in that situation?

I had called ahead to make sure that it was okay to have visitors, and when I got there Luke wasn't there. His wife told me that right after he got off the phone with me, he'd grabbed his coat and rushed out. He said he was going to his office to write; some story he'd been working on. He said he needed to make some changes, that it was urgent, it couldn't wait. She told me that it was his way of coping. He hadn't been handling the whole situation well at all, he was completely distraught and she thought it might be good for him to do some writing, as a release. I said I agreed, and walked over to the bed where his daughter lay, ghostly pale and unconscious. I set some flowers by her bedside and looked down at her. She had wires and tubes running in and out of her from all angles. I couldn't imagine the anguish that Luke must have been feeling now, to see his daughter this way.

Then very suddenly he burst into the room and thrust a handful of typewritten pages in my face. He was disheveled and frantic. His eyes were bloodshot and hysterical-looking. "Read it!" he told me, practically shoving the papers down my shirt. I felt defensive, not sure what he meant by acting this way. I didn't know if he was angry at me or if he had written some sort of suicide note and I was to be his final witness, but I took the papers and read the first few lines, then I remembered. It was the story we'd discussed the last time I saw him. I looked up at him, still unsure of what his intentions were, but now in his eyes I could see desperation. He looked at me with all of the anguish of a man whose daughter lay dying and who had come to the end of his hope, and was now asking for a miracle. I read the story again, exactly as it was the first time only now the ending was different.

That was as much as my friend had written thus far, but he assured me that the miracle which the man was so desperate for, willing to destruct his entire belief system for, was granted, and in the end the girl lived.

Fran Gruenhaupt

The Hired Man

The lanky figure took long strides across the snowy barnyard. In one hand he held his rifle and in the other he held the hind legs of three rabbits. I stood at the kitchen window waiting for Noah to open the outside basement door. As soon as he started down the steps, I ran to the inside cellar door in our kitchen and rushed down to greet him. I liked to watch him skin the rabbits and gut them.

After tossing the rabbits on the floor, he removed his worn jacket, hanging it on the hook on the center post near his old wooden chair. The rifle was hung on a rack on the wall. It was cool in the basement, but Noah wore long underwear and heavy overalls to keep him warm. I stayed with him while he cleaned the rabbits, talking to him and asking questions while he quietly went about his work. His one-or two-word answers to my questions satisfied me. The silence between us was comfortable.

Noah placed old newspapers on the floor, found his hunting knife, and placed the three rabbits side-by-side on the paper. Sitting in his creaky chair, Noah leaned over to work on the rabbits. He carefully slit the rabbit's leg skin until he was able to undress the rabbit as if he was pulling a sweater off. Smooth pink meat underneath showed all the muscles. It was beautiful to see, almost like a picture in a textbook. Noah worked only a few minutes and all three rabbits were skinned.

After gutting the rabbits, Noah cleaned them under cold water until the water was clear and the rabbits were ready for Mom. Noah and I climbed the wooden basement steps and delivered the rabbits to Mom. I knew that she would cook them with gravy and potatoes in the next day or two.

Noah often hunted rabbits, pheasants, squirrels, or anything in season. Mom cooked it all. And I enjoyed eating whatever he caught. After any hunting trip, whether short or long, Noah spent hours cleaning and polishing his guns. I watched as he gathered the oil and tore the rags, fascinated with how many times he put the little cleaning rag through the gun and how much time he spent polishing the wooden gun stock. The guns were well cared for. I believe now that they must have been his most valuable possessions. Noah did not have many worldly possessions.

Noah McKinney lived in our home all of the time I was growing up. He came to Mom and Dad's as a middle-aged hired man before I was born. He left as an old man after I started college. The west bedroom was always Noah's room just as the large wooden leather-seated rocking chair in the north end of the dining room was his chair. Noah never married and he never owned or drove a car. His best friends, Harry Haling and Raymond Linn, were his hunting and fishing buddies who took him with them on yearly vacations to fish in Canada.

As a child I could not understand why Noah was not a relative. He was there for every family event, including births, baptisms, anniversaries, and graduations. And yet, he wasn't there. He didn't go to church with us, he didn't dress up for the parties, and he often disappeared to the basement when company came. Yet our home was his only home. Our dining room table was his dinner table just as it was ours. And he enjoyed immensely the meals that Mom prepared as he ate heartily and never gained an ounce of fat on his lean frame.

Noah appeared to be happy, but he was a quiet person, seldom hurried, and never speaking loudly. I loved Noah because he listened to me and never said a cross word to me when I tagged along. He didn't always have patience with straying cows or wandering pigs, but he always had patience with me. In his spare time, especially on cold days in the winter, he would sit near the warm furnace in the basement and whittle. I liked the whistles he made and the little figures he carved. In the evenings he often sat in the dining room after supper, reading The Des Moines Register and, eventually, falling asleep with the newspaper in his hands.

Noah's job was to assist with the farm chores on our 240-acre dairy farm. This meant arising for chores about 4:30 or 5 a.m. each day, all year long and in all kinds of weather. He trudged down the lane to the field with our dog to round up the cattle for milking time. Dirt and sweat never seemed to bother Noah, but the summer heat slowed him down. The work was not always easy, but Noah was steady and solid. He was not a leader, not one to enjoy making decisions, but he worked hard. It seemed to me that he and Dad had a good working relationship, almost knowing what each one would do without any words passing between them. His help made farm life easier for Mom and Dad during the years he worked for them.

Noah came from Missouri to Grundy County, Iowa, to work on farms, helping on several different farms prior to being hired by Dad. Mom and Dad gave him the small west bedroom with a large walk-in closet, a single bed, and a chest of drawers. His wardrobe included only the basics and three or four pairs of dark blue bib overalls and blue work shirts, laundered, mended, and patched by Mom. The tall, slender man hung a mirror on the post in the basement and lathered and shaved every few days, sometimes under the watchful eye of my sister and myself. He knew our family well, yet he seldom voiced his opinions.

In our home Noah was just always there. We gave him presents at Christmas, but he seldom participated in the festivities except for the dining. I can't imagine our home without him, and almost every memory I have of events on the farm has Noah somewhere in the activities. I remember vividly one time when I feared that Noah had been injured.

One evening when Noah was sitting peacefully in his chair in the dining room, he got the surprise of his life. Outdoors a summer thunderstorm was in full bloom, lightning streaking up and down and thunder cracks shaking the house. Mom and Dad, Carolyn and I were all in the living and dining room area when a sudden quiet pause broke into a fireball around the old brown telephone attached to the wall just above Noah's head. The lightning and the explosive boom of the thunder were almost simultaneous. It was followed instantly by the shock of total darkness. The putrid odor of burning wires filled the room as Mom scrambled to find a flashlight. Amid the confusion we discovered that the telephone had been knocked off the wall right behind Noah's head. It had been replaced by a large sooty burned spot. Noah, the person closest to the ball of fire, was very calm, but the rest of us were almost hysterical. No one was injured, but none of us ever forgot that night in our dining room.

As the years went by Noah's tall strong body became a little bent, his hair thinned and grayed, and his well tanned face became leathery and lined with wrinkles. Work on the dairy farm was the only life he knew, and I believe he loved it. When Dad did not have the dairy cows and did not need a hired man, Noah returned to Missouri to his sister's home. I was in college and never said goodbye to him. He was not one to write or call, and we never heard from him again.

As an adult I have thought about Noah and the life he lived. We were his family, and he had so few material possessions. Was he happy? I hope so. I knew him, and yet I didn't know him. Growing up on the farm would not have been the same without this gentle hired man.

Terry Wahls

Sons and Daughters

He tells me I have to sign the papers, but I do not want to do it. Those two red short horns with heifer calves are mine. So what if I am only in seventh grade. Grandpa transferred the ownership of those cows and calves to me, Terry L. Wahls.

Last year my father was all smiles when grandpa gave my brothers and me two cows, each, for promising to wait until we were 21 before drinking any alcohol. This year however, he is always complaining about all the grass our cows are eating. Just what did they eat last year, imaginary grass?

Sitting at the table, pointedly ignoring him, I pull my pencil across the paper, staring intently at the pitcher of wooden spoons. My older brother Rick bumps the table, ruining my lines.

I do not look at him, instead I start erasing the errant marks. Then Rick pulls my shoulder, and says, "Can't you hear the old man?"

I resume drawing, still saying nothing. Rick grumbles, "We won't get to do anything until you sign!" and knocks the table again.

Glaring at him, I stop drawing, pick up my notebook and pencil, walk into the living room, and sit down on the tattered couch. My dad is six feet tall, and since quitting smoking, his belly is now as big as his chest. Shaving only two or three times a week, he nearly always has some stubble on his face, which is darkly tanned from hours in the sun.

He thrusts a couple catalogs at me, telling me to look them over. Dutifully I begin flipping the pages.

Hmm, whose semen should I order today? Should it be from the red bull, with the massive head and shoulders? He has a big trophy, 89 percent success rate at settling the cows that is making them pregnant. His offspring have quite a number of awards listed. On the other hand, what about the strawberry roan? He has good statistics too.

"Look over the names of the owners, Terry," commands my dad.

He is right, they are all farmer John, or David, or Robert, occasionally with "and Sons" tacked on at the end.

Throwing the catalog to the floor, I stand up, and mutter, "So what if no one else does. Why can't you use, John Wahls and Family?"

His reply is crisp, loud, and final. "No one else does it that way, and I am not going to either!"

I stand. Slowly, quietly I say, "You might wish I was your son, but I'm not!"

Turning my back on him, I walk out, slamming the screen door.

Joseph M. Petrick

Workaday

I think the door is broken. I'm standing behind the register at the Kum and Go Gas Station, and I'm counting the number of times the little bell rings as someone enters or exits the store. Normally it's just the once. A kind of a doorbell type sound. Still the familiar "bing-bong" chime but more electronic, like an impression of a doorbell made by a digital watch. Also you don't have to press anything to hear it. You just walk in or out. Like I said, usually the bell only rings once but when working an eight hour shift, once is plenty and today every time someone steps through the door it goes "bing-bong bing-bong bing-bong."

"It's been like this since three," I say to Patrick, my manager. "Some old guy in a wheelchair was having trouble getting through the door; the bell just kept going off, again and again and ever since it's been like this. Do you think you could fix it?" I ask.

"Dunno. I'll call a guy and have him check it out on Monday," he says, with as much authority as he can muster on the subject of mechanical know-how. As though offhandedly referring to some nameless man will assuage my annoyance. A small part of me considers inquiring further as to just who this "guy" would be and whether he went to some kind of university to acquire his vast knowledge of electronic doorbell repair or if it was just a course he took at The Learning Annex. But then, that would require voluntarily communicating with Patrick, which is something I've learned to avoid as much as possible, due mostly to my lack of interest in either NASCAR or chewing tobacco products, for which Patrick seems to have an uncanny ability to segue any conversation into if given even a few brief sentences with which to navigate.

I've been here eight months now. The same eight months since I dropped out of school. At the time it felt like a good idea, smart even. Get a job and make money. Money for an eventual apartment, eventual car payments, eventual cable TV with eventual dirty channels. Start to live my life, whatever that means. Be like ... a citizen with a job, not just a kid with a diploma, all wide-eyed and full of optimism. Because we can't ALL be doctors, we can't ALL be lawyers and firemen, we were taught to dream of noble goals. What they didn't tell us was that not everyone gets their wish. Some may just drop out and get a shitty job at a gas station.

When you work at a gas station people tend to lose any qualities of individuality from one another. They simply join their rank in a kind of short lineup of regulars. Frat boys begging to be sold beer past 2 a.m. after all the bars have closed. There could be 50 of them one night or there could be one. It wouldn't matter. They might all sport a variety of different colognes but the fact that they all stink of wearing too much of it binds them together. Broke college kids who spent all their allowance on weed and then pay for $3.50 of gas in pennies inevitably sort their change out on the counter, carefully picking out the stems that linger in their pockets and rejoicing at the discovery of a silver coin will become faceless in a surprisingly short amount of time. While these people may think they live their own, separate, interesting, maybe even important lives, to me they're just another in a long line of poor imitations of themselves. Like a Halloween party where everyone accidentally wore the same masks, their vague semblance of identity will never supersede the overall stereotype that is their lives.

That's what's great about this job, because you do the judging. You ring up their Mountain Dew and their Marlboro Reds and say "have a nice day" and all from the safety of your little box behind the register, away from the quiet, needling possibility that you too could fit into one of these groups.

It's almost seven. Right about now is when the used car guys get off work. In the morning they buy coffee and Maxim and Visine, recounting their stories of the previous night's X-rated mischief. At noon they buy Red Bull and microwave burritos and bullshit with the bicycle cops. Soon they'll be here for scratch-off tickets, taking their sweet time to delicately decide which particular cards they will waste their money on today and act as though there is a science to their idiocy. As though luck and mathematics had worked out some kind of harmonic deal just for them.

"Gimmie uh ... hmm ... uh ... gimmie ... two 'Gobs and Gobs' and a 'Pot O' Gold' and three 'Money Trees.'" If there is a certain indignity to leaving a convenience store with the knowledge that you've blown $50 on a scratch-off game called "Biggie Bucks," then these guys are impervious to it. As well as to the irony of blowing half a paycheck on a game called "Easy Money" and walking away with only a ten-dollar winner.

These guys make it a point to know your name and they love to use it. "JIMMY-JIMMY-JIMMY!" they yell excitedly upon entrance. "Whacha got for me today? A winner? I want me a winner, Jimmy!" And you can't help but feel sorry for them, because truly, this is their only form of intimacy. Because their view of romance includes little nuggets of advice like the fact that some strippers, if you give them even just a LITTLE bit of coke, will totally do anything for you. Anything.

Worst of all though, is the fact that while you're paid to be here all day long, they come in of their own free will. They choose to know our duty schedule and memorize the price of a refill for a 64-ounce "cup" of coffee. So you humor them and laugh at their stupid jokes about blondes and Polish people and Michael Jackson. You smile when they enter and wave goodbye when they leave but secretly you worry that a pathetic existence is some how contagious.

"Bing-bong bing-bong bing-bong." A homeless man enters with a bag of dirty cans he's pulled from every gutter and dumpster in town. He smiles a toothless yellow grin and for a moment I wonder if he's secretly a genius. Dressed in rags, he would spout poetic ramblings and recite Nietzsche or Tolstoy and wax intellectually about the materialistic nature of our society and other profundities concerning our addiction to "stuff." Maybe he'd look at me and immediately notice that I was special. That I was somehow above this place and these people. We'd become friends, our relationship growing to that of a mentor and his pupil and culminating with a dramatic heart attack, leaving him dying in my arms and reminding me breathlessly that through it all, life moves far too fast and should be cherished — to never forget to live every moment like it's my last.

The man belches and adjusts his "Beaver University" baseball cap, and I decide that perhaps I need to watch fewer Hallmark Original Movies.

I count out his cans, each rattling with damp cigarette butts like the marbles in so many spray paint canisters and ring up four dollars. He brings over two 40 ounce bottles of "Miller High Life" and I do my best not to find the situation more than a little humorous. Why the cheapest beer is called "High Life" I will never fully understand. "Colt 45" makes sense. The "Silver Bullet" would also be an appropriate moniker for a tool used most commonly to dull the pain of one's miserable life. But, isn't "High Life" a smack in the face to anyone destitute enough to purchase it? Before I can make up my mind it's, "bing-bong bing-bong bing-bong," and my penniless mentor is gone.

There are worse jobs to have in the world. There must be. Any job where you are forced to wear a stupid hat or chirp mindless slogans when you sell a McWhatever would qualify. Such phrases might include "Have a burger-licious day!" and "thanks again and remember that here at the Taco Hut, it's always a fiesta!" Other jobs on the list are as follows: telemarketer, complaint supervisor for a computer company and "the guy who cleans up aisle five." These are jobs where the best day one can hope for is only slightly less shitty than the worst. "I was only called an asshole twelve times today!" or, "At least this time it was only pee," might be a jubilant huzzah for some, but for me, only further proof that even the promise of a steady paycheck can have its limits.

If I had stayed in school I would have graduated today. This is the sort of thinking that gets you into trouble when you have a job at a gas station. Looking back day-to-day, recounting the mistakes you've made, it's enough to make you wonder why they don't take your belt and shoelaces away when they hire you.

"Is this really my life?" In the quiet moments between the self-righteous judgments of our patrons, I've found that question staring me in the face more often than I had expected when I dropped off the application. People compromise, that's what they do. Some guys work their whole lives as mailmen and insurance salesman and janitors. Did they dream of it in their youth? Of course not. But somewhere along the line their dream of being an astronaut or a professional wrestler went south and this is their second place. A consolation in the form of a weekly pay stub and all the alcohol it takes to make them forget the hours that it represents.

Yet, there are happy people. Who am I to say that just because a guy is a janitor he's miserable? What gives me the right to say that's not exactly where he wants to be? Maybe he has a wife and kids that he loves and that he enjoys bringing a paycheck home to. Maybe he has a hobby, something that he enjoys doing. Or maybe he still dreams of something better, something he's been saving for all his life. He could be the first man to invent an affordable jet pack or a cleaner burning fuel. Something that could really help the world, improve it even. Who says that a man's life, his worth, his entire being is dictated by his job?

I have this argument with myself every so often. Sometimes, the idealist wins and I decide that this is only temporary. It is a transition between the past and the future that I'm bound to be meant for; the prologue to the biography of my life and to all the adventures and wisdom that is contained within its pages. Other times, these far more frequent, the cynic in me wins, and I resign myself to a destiny where all the numbers end in nine and every magazine has 108 more ways to arouse your partner.

The bell rings its familiar harassment and I find myself greeted by familiar faces and a dress code suitable for photos with Grandma.

"Hey Jim," says Will, an old friend of a friend with a smile so sickeningly sweet you expect it to come with a badge that reads: WELCOME TO WALMART.

"Hi," I say and toss a smile to his girlfriend whose name I never bothered learning but with friends referred to as "Toothy."

"You working tonight?" he asks. "I'm sorry, that was dumb, obviously you're working."

"Yup," I say. "Did you just get back from graduation?"

"Yeah. My mom had a dinner thing we went to after. Now we're just ... hanging out," he says. "You got any plans once you get off?"

"Umm, not really, no."

"Well hey, we're going to a party over at Weaver's place, you should come!"

I think this over for a moment, which is all it takes for me to decide that "Mitch Weaver's celebratory beer bust" is perhaps the very last place that I would like to be tonight. I can't be sure of this however, because there are so many horrible places that I've never been: A Vietnamese P.O.W. camp for example. Still, for all I can imagine, it's hard not to assume that I would still rather hear the shrill command of "Didi Mow!" than "CHUG! CHUG! CHUG!"

"Yeah, maybe," I say.

"Cool man. I'll see you there."

Then before I know it, "bing-bong bing-bong bing-bong," and both Walmart and Toothy are gone.

I never should have dropped out. Seeing their faces, their bright, hopeful faces and it's clear to me now. I wonder if there's still time to get my shit together. Maybe get my G.E.D. Maybe figure out something that I actually like doing and would enjoy devoting myself to.

But then ... no. One could devote an entire lifetime to something only to watch it fail and I just don't know if I could handle that kind of rejection — be it destiny, fate or otherwise.

In the end, maybe it's better to just move with life like an unmanned boat in the ocean. Why fight the current? Why not just allow it to take you through the seasons, enjoying the simple pleasures as they drift past: music, movies, good friends, girlfriends.

I should be a Buddhist. I bet I'd be a good one. I could be like "Super Buddhist" and when I arrive at the temple, the wise, old, leader of the monks would look at me and just know that I would barely even need any training because I already knew so much instinctively. Even the karate skills would probably just come naturally. Then maybe I'd just wander the earth, sleeping under bridges, solving the occasional crime and seducing women with my wise, yet simple credos about beauty and truth.

When I'd leave them, they'd beg me not to go, sobbing:

"But Master! I've so much left to learn!" But I'd just turn to them dramatically and say something like: "The only lessons that remain are the ones you must teach yourself." Then a gust of wind and I'd blow away like dust.

Yeah, I'd like that. But there really aren't any Buddhist monasteries around Iowa City.

At least, none that I know of.

I wonder who I could have been if I hadn't been born as me. Whose eyes would I have been looking through, seeing through. Maybe if I'd just made different choices.

I once saw a movie in which Bill Murray had to repeat the same day over and over again. At first he didn't understand what was going on but gradually he began to accept the reality of his situation and enjoy the meaninglessness of it. He took chances and risks without a second thought because he knew that he wouldn't face any consequences and cultivated a number of different personalities because regardless of whether he was a wonderful, giving, gentle man or a greedy, mean spirited jerk — each day he would wake up to Sonny and Cher singing "I Got You Babe," knowing that none of it mattered. In many ways I related to his struggle because for me, as the days go on, they begin to look so similar to the each other that it's getting harder and harder to tell them apart. Am I stuck in a similar conundrum? Is my life becoming some kind of sick, skipping record?

I think this and I begin to wonder how much cash might sit in the register at this exact moment. I imagine myself, taking the money, leaving the store and just running away. Who would I be then? Whose eyes would I see through then? Would I wake up tomorrow morning to the tune of "I Got You Babe" or would something ... change?

I can almost feel the money in my hands. The sweaty, wrinkled dollars, gripped tightly in my fist, their starchy texture wilting within my clenched fingers. I can almost see their faces, George Washington, Andrew Jackson, Ulysses S. Grant and under the drawer, Benjamin Franklin, all smiling and cheering me on in charming British accents.

"This is the right thing to do!" says George Washington. "And I cannot tell a lie!"

Then, out of nowhere it hits me. Somehow, without really even knowing how I got here, I stand in front of the open register. I hold a small wad of bills. Suddenly my breath is short. I'm sweating. I feel every single nerve in my body, standing on end. My eyelids, heavy, like the giant curtains of a Broadway show, begging to sweep closed to uproarious applause. My heart feels like it's beating at a million miles an hour and yet everything feels like it's moving in slow motion. I curl my toes into fists within my shoes and I let the curtains fall. I see the words: RUN. LEAVE. GET OUT. ESCAPE. I see them in the darkness and I hear my mind agree.

I take in a breath. I wait.

And then ... and then ... and then ....

I exhale. I shake off the haze and I open my eyes. I wait for my heart to slow to an unmedicated pace. I quietly put the money back. It fits snugly into the drawer, like making a tiny bed with many blankets. I close the drawer and listen for the satisfying echo of its lock. I run my fingers through my hair and I put my hands on the counter. I look at them, study them. They are mine. My hands. They belong to me. This is my life. My life. This.

I blink once. Then again.

"Bing-bong bing-bong bing-bong."
"Bing-bong bing-bong bing-bong."

I look up. A child, probably no older than six is opening the door and marveling at the resulting sound. He closes it ... and then opens it again.

"Bing-bong bing-bong bing-bong."

He smiles, enchanted.

"Bing-bong bing-bong bing-bong."
"Bing-bong bing-bong bing-bong."
"Bing-bong bing-bong bing-bong."

Corinne Stanley

Transgression

Who will catch the floating bodies
traveling on the weary Tigris?

Women in embroidered shadows
mouth their soundless rage.

Men with missing appendages
crawl aimlessly with ghosts.

Who will catch the floating bodies?

We, the fishers of dead things,
carrying our nets of iron will.

We, the emboldened liars,
blinded by black avarice —

we will catch the bloated wrongs
of our transgressions.

Woe to us
who sit in interior rooms
and fiddle with plastic distractions.

Woe to me
who writes on yellow paper
a shabby concession to contrite moments.

Who will catch the floating bodies
working their way to the source
of the once mighty River?

Mary Vermillion

The Cereal Aisle

■ ■ ■

She is doing the best that she can. A loving thing, really. That's what Judy tells herself as she sets her baby — carrier and all — in the grocery cart. Some couple who totally love each other and never need food stamps will find him and raise him as their own.

The cereal aisle is empty except for an old man with a wad of coupons and a calculator. Judy waits for him to leave. He stretches toward the top shelf, grasps a box of Raisin Bran, and begins shuffling to the next aisle. Then he stops and fiddles with his calculator. What is he doing? Algebra? Soon the store will fill with shoppers on their way home from work. Judy needs to get out of there. She adjusts her baby's blanket, the man turns his back, and Judy dashes away, her ponytail swinging back and forth.

■

Violet struggles with her cart's wayward front wheel. She checks her list and peers through bifocals at a box of Cheerios. (New study indicates that as part of a heart-healthy diet Cheerios can help reduce cholesterol!) She will not let Bill have another heart attack. This last one nearly killed her. She nudges a cart that blocks her way to the Bran Buds. What an adorable baby! A wee bit of blonde hair, peach fuzz, Bill calls it. What kind of mother would leave an infant unattended? Violet is not surprised when three girls — all laughter, ratty jeans, frizzy hair, and clunky shoes — stride down the aisle. The blonde one — probably the mother — has a ring in her nose and a 12-pack of beer in her arms.

■

The cereal aisle swarms with women who have abandoned their high heels for tennis shoes. Naomi envies their tackiness. She forgot her sneakers, and her feet ache. Her hose are snagged, and the underarms of her blouse stained with perspiration. She has two hours to get groceries, pick up the kids, clean the house, and prepare dinner for her in-laws. Her sister's wedding is two weeks away, and Naomi still hasn't lost any weight. Not an ounce. Grabbing the Special K, she hears a baby whimper. Thank God she didn't have to bring her kids to the store.

Edgar hates backtracking, but it has to be done. He lost his Raisin Bran coupon, so he needs to find a cheaper cereal. As he pulls his calculator out of his shirt pocket, a lady whisks by, high heels clicking. Pretty and plump like Hetty before the cancer. Where are the generic Rice Krispies? Edgar could use some snap, crackle, pop. Steering through a maze of carts, he glances down and sees a baby. Lordamighty. Kid needs its diaper changed.

Jack's thighs cramp from cross country practice, and his stomach growls. Alison will never go out with him. She is probably getting ready for a date with some other guy while Jack marks price reductions in the cereal aisle. It seems extra long tonight — empty except for a cart at the far end. As he loosens his tie and gazes at Count Chocula, a baby starts wailing. Jack glares at the unattended cart. The wailing increases, so he flees to the freezer section.

Lynne isn't bothered by the baby's smell. She grips a box of Product 19 and stares at the crying child. When she miscarried this time, she was six months along, and David was refinishing an antique cradle. It will be years before they can adopt because he insists on a healthy white infant. This baby is darling, even with its scrunched, red face. She longs to hold it close, but what if its mother catches her?

Andrea tries to breathe through her mouth as she hunts for low-fat granola. The cereal aisle really stinks. She should speak to the manager, but she wants to get home and tell Sam about her promotion. She beat out five men — two of them with MBAs! Sam will brag about her at their dinner party tonight, and she will modestly accept everyone's congratulations. Andrea checks her cart — wine, salmon, risotto, asparagus, bread — all she needs is dessert. Weighing the relative merits of chocolate mousse and raspberry sorbet, she hurries past a crying baby. So that's what stinks. Why doesn't its mother do something instead of just standing there hugging a box of cereal?

Caitlin clutches the doll she got in her cheeseburger Happy Meal. She and Daddy eat at MacDonald's all the time since Mommy moved away. Through the bars of a cart, she studies a baby. It smells like poop, and it is crying hard, kicking its legs. Caitlin asks her daddy why the baby is crying, but he doesn't answer. Louder, she asks if they can please buy some Frosted Flakes, wanting him to joke about the Cavity Bug (who loves little-girl teeth best of all), but he simply nods and rounds the corner. She bolts after him, forgetting all about the cereal and the baby.

Mattie frantically searches for Crispix. Her left arm is in a sling, so when she tries to maneuver between two carts, she bumps the one with a baby. It needs a fresh diaper. It hiccups, and its eyes dart around. She must have scared it. "There, there," she coos. "You're okay — all safe and sound." To the right of the baby, she spies the Crispix and relaxes. Last time she couldn't find Greg's favorite he gave her a black eye.

Jack shivers as he leaves the freezer section for the cereal aisle. Quiet. No customers, only a partially filled cart. But wait. There's a baby. It can't be same one that was bawling before. No way. But he should check with someone just in case — he knows he should — but last night when he was talking to Alison in the produce section, his manager warned him to Stay On Task or Look For Another Job. Jack turns from the cart and faces a wall of boxes: Blueberry Morning, Lucky Charms, Just Right, Smart Start, Healthy Choice. There is a lot of work to do.

Liz Lynn Miller

Lauds

Just then

because the over-warm morning
was so much the child
of weighty, unrelieved night

and because it was,
after all,
past time good people should rise

and because a Pius or perhaps a Sixtus
so far away in his sequestered city
so many centuries past
decreed it done, and done even now

just then

a shred of breeze
a sweet zephyr
swirled among the newsy finches
and jays, catbirds, robins and wrens
busy
so busy with May-time work
even this early, this warm

that breeze which rippled their feathers,
that breeze kicked to life
a neighbor's bass chimes
and the altos of another

and yes, just then

the angelus sounded at St. Meg's,
calling notice
to that wind we'd so wanted
since last evening,
lifting us from sleep at last
to take for ourselves another day.

Gerine Tenold

Psychedelia

Imitation of John Milton's Paradise Lost 7.387-416

And Psychedelia said, "Let the airwaves bring forth
Beatles with hits uncountable, soaring 45s:
And let winged Byrds fly eight miles high
Suspended in the starry hall of fame."
And Psychedelia produced the great Turtles, and each
Soaring 45, each that reeled, which explosively
The airwaves reverberated according to their styles.
And every Iron Butterfly after his kind:
And knew that it was groovy and promoted them, singing,
"Be Mamas and Papas, and in the cities
And suburbs and growing towns the airwaves fill:
And let party Animals teem under the rising sun."
Henceforth Motown and Apple and Columbia and RCA
With progeny uncountable produce, and throngs
Of hippies with granny glasses and tie-dyed shirts
Sway like waves under blue-sky stadiums that oft
Signify a park: some alone or with friends
Groove on Grassroots their pasture, and through Doors
Of solid gold stray, or sporting with dazed stare
Show to the sunny afternoon Kinky shirts,
Or in their flowery bell-bottoms at ease, await
Soul food, or from Rolling Stones their satisfaction
In spaced out fashion seek: on smooth the Spoonful,
And Mindbenders play: part (Se)bastion of rock
Tripping uncannily, dreamy in their stride
Tempest the stage: there Steppenwolf
Most monolithic hairy creatures, in the Wild
Spread out like stone-henge, stands by or thunders,
And seems a shifting gibraltar, and at their mikes
Suck in, and at their speakers roar out the 60s.

Shauna Banning
Centers

I questioned
how
she spun 'round
so fast
without ever
falling down.

I watched
again
as she extended
outward arms
and upward eyes.
Her center
appeared to
multiply itself out
to infinity.
"Simple,"
she said.

"You cannot be afraid
of gravity."

Jason Bengtson

The Woods of Fall

Sam tapped his cigarette against the sole of his shoe. In the darkness, between the tall, groping trees, the sparks fell like a shower of stars.

"Nice, here," he said, as if to no one in particular, which David appreciated. He appreciated a lot of things about Sam. His slow smile, his calm eyes, but most of all David appreciated his strange and quiet ways.

"Yes," David responded softly, through a swollen throat.

"He'd have liked it here. Like when we took them all camping. You remember. He always liked the trees. The growing things."

"Yes. He did."

In the darkness of the woods the constant reality of survival played itself out. Animals prowled and cried out and were silenced. David thought he could hear each one of them breathing.

"Is it finished?"

David turned to him, not comprehending, struggling for his friend's meaning.

"What ...?"

"Did you empty it out? Where he wanted it?"

"He never said. Not exactly. But when they're a boy, who thinks ... but I ... but yes, it's done."

"Then you should come back to the camp, Dave. Come back to the fire."

"My dad first took me up here when I was seven. Did you know that? I was just a boy myself then. I used to roam all around these woods. I could walk them in the dark. I wonder. I wonder if I could still find my way."

"You shouldn't do that."

"Why? Why not?"

"You'd get lost, Dave. Time changes things."

"You know I never got hurt up here. Not once in all those years. Camping and hunting and fishing all those years and it was like a dream. Can you understand that? Do you understand how it can be that way?"

Something tight and heavy choked off the end of the sentence. Sam put his hand on his friend's shoulder. It felt bent, hollow, defeated.

"Come back to the fire. They're all waiting for you."

"No. Not yet. You go on. You tell them ... tell them I'll be back soon."

Sam exhaled a gout of pale smoke.

"Sure. I'll tell them. But don't stay up too long."

Leaves rustled underfoot as Sam started toward the camp, then stopped. There was silence. When Sam finally spoke again he sounded different. Softer.

"It wasn't your fault, you know. It really wasn't. It might have been God's fault, but it surely wasn't yours."

David felt something thin and hard battering itself against the inside of his chest. He felt his throat close up and he couldn't answer. Couldn't think of how to answer. The words that he wanted to find escaped his reach, danced about his head like the sound of young, drifting laughter, and a moment later Sam started off along the path, leaving him alone.

The sob caught David by surprise, took him to his knees and wracked his body. The floor of the forest was cool and disinterested. It was littered with leaves and branches in the wanton disorder of a young child's room. David heard Sam's footsteps in the dark distance and he thanked him for not stopping, thanked him beneath his terrible lurching sobs.

The forest, with its myriad of life, was still a graveyard. Under every footfall lay the remains of those that had lived before, dismal and abundant. David reached his hands out, bent over like a penitent, fingers straining, before dropping them to the earth and scooping the detritus of the forest floor back toward him, now a man trying to gather up and remake the past. He felt suddenly, in that instant, that he could fix it. That there was some way that he could reshape the loamy soil and the moist leaves into something warm and definite and human. It seemed that it could be a simple thing, a small thing really, to push time backwards and remake all of the things that had become broken.

The momentary reverie passed, leaving David clutching the soggy remnants of the forest's entropy. He clenched his handfuls desperately, hopelessly, a numbness beginning to creep into his fingers. Overhead the trees swayed as a bone-chilling autumn wind whipped through the branches and, still lower, shifted the saturated contents of the forest floor. David lifted up his hands and opened them, leaving the pulpy masses of twigs and filthy leaves to fall down around him. They were limp and vaguely pathetic.

It will be this moment, he decided, it will be now, in the dark, when all delusions fall away and all lights go out. I will live here, and I will not be able to escape. I will wilt, like these dead leaves. I will lose my color and my firmness and everything within me will fall to rot. When I move it will be like the creeping movement of the smallest, strangest thing. And when I lay down it will be as ashes falling onto the earth. Those who love me will learn to love my absence, because I now have nothing else for them.

The wind arced beneath the collar of his jacket, racing along David's bare skin with what should have been a bracing shock. But, despite an involuntary shudder, David found that he felt nothing. The cold was swallowed up within him, tossed into a black pit with the rest of his sensations, feeding an emptiness that filled him completely.

He stood reluctantly, because he could think of nothing else to do. His narrow hands with their long, fluttering fingers brushed his trousers off and for a moment he simply stood, a slim figure drooping pointlessly among the hulking trunks. He finally started off toward camp, gathering the impetus to accelerate to a slow, stumbling walk after a few listless steps. As he moved along the trail, he found himself hoping only one thing. He hoped Sam was wrong.

He hoped that he would find no one waiting for him.

Liz Lynn Miller

Menu

On the grill this morning's catch
is sizzling as his friends array themselves

at points circling the patio, and overhead
altocumulus swim across the late-day sky

like fish bones — ribs and spine — leaping
westward, tail-end arcing and diminishing

while orange sun pools at the horizon.
The crisp-edged fish is dished and passed,

and guests up-turn bottles of lager, ale and stout
between forking flakes of catfish

from chains of bones. Soon enough the clouds
re-school as rows of gold-rimmed puffs.

And over the steady coals guests toast
marshmallows, cautiously bite caramel skins

from ethereal interiors, wipe sticky hands
on cool grass, then settle in for an evening

of clouds unveiling and veiling planets,
moon, and stars, hide and seeking.

Linda N. Woito

To a Woman's Skinny Soul

She's sorry she left it
out under the porch with the dogs too long
sorry she forgot to feed it
at noon, when she fed the cats the sheep the goats the pigs
in the barn, snuggling together like animals do
— they know a storm is coming
blizzard tornado they head to the barn

now she says she's sorry she left it, her Skinny Soul
out in the cold
stringing tulips on a rope
given to her by her friend Janusz
who survived Russian gulags

now she asks — why did she refuse his kiss
that night
— was it because his hands were too rough
clumsy for a famous plastic surgeon?

after he came back, after he studied
medicine, his hands worked miracles
on children's faces
put their lips together so they could smile —
maybe Janusz should work on it — her Skinny Soul
standing outside on the balcony, reed-thin like Janusz himself
when he returned from the gulags

he should have been too weak to care —
he should have been too weak to care about
faces and lips of children
that skinny-souled woman,

calves crying in the night, out behind the barn
back in the gulags — like when she
refused his kiss, like when they forgot to feed him
in the gulags
because they thought
he was just another dog howling in the night.

Chris Kilgore

The Immovable Object vs. The Unstoppable Force

■ ■ ■

This summer I was traveling through the southwest and the border region on an education grant, collecting the folk tales and oral histories of the people that lived there, especially those whose families had lived there for generations. Most of the stories were what you would expect and similar to the oral history of any culture. But there was one story unlike any I have ever heard, that in a particular region of southern Arizona and down past the border near Nogales, I heard told many times by many disparate people, in many different ways. This was the story of The Immovable Object against The Unstoppable Force.

That this story, regardless of where I heard it, always bore the title of the famous paradox was entirely coincidental. The Immovable Object and The Unstoppable Force, in this story were not hypothetical entities, but real people, combatants in the contest, known throughout this region as "mirando del alma," which in most places in the U.S. is casually referred to as a stare down, the object being to maintain eye contact with your opponent until one or the other blinked or looked away. Here we think of this as something of a children's game, and although even in that area, the sport had faded away to the point where only the old men could attest to ever having actually seen a contest, it had once been a game of great importance. To sit face to face with an opponent and lock eyes was considered the ultimate test of a man's machismo. It was taken for granted that the eyes were windows into the soul, and so two "lookers," which is what the combatants were called, facing each other with their souls bared were making war in a spiritual dimension, on a level that couldn't be reached with a knife or a pistol. With such conventional weapons a man could be wounded in body, even killed, but the soul would remain untouched. In "mirando del alma" a man could break the very essence of his opponent. In addition, a weak-willed man could not hide behind technology, physical strength or even intelligence, only the true might of his spirit would determine whether he could succeed or fail, it was the only true measure of a man.

"The Immovable Object" and "The Unstoppable Force" were the names of the two most legendary "lookers" in the history of "mirando del alma." The story that I was told in so many ways so many times was the recounting of the match in which they faced each other, two legends face to face, soul to soul. The most compelling, and in my personal opinion, the most reliable version of the story was told to me one night by an old man, with a dark, leathery face, dressed in rags at a small tavern in Rio Rico Arizona, just a few miles north of the Mexico border.

He approached the table where I sat with three other men, all of them in their late 30s, third- or fourth-generation ranchers and cattlemen who were all giving me their various renditions of the story and bickering over details and whose story was more accurate. The old man pulled up a chair to the table, uninvited, somewhat to the chagrin of the younger men already there. He told me that each of their versions of the story were bunk and that his was the only authoritative version of the story, because he had actually been there, and seen the contest take place. The other men said he was full of shit, and crazy. They said the story took place more than 200 years ago, and so he must be lying. I was still interested as I had heard varying dates, ranging from before the Spanish American war to only 10 or 15 years ago. About that time, the three men who I'd been talking to determined it was time to leave, likely as much from the filth of the old man as the insulting way in which he talked to them, which they didn't appreciate seeing as he was a tramp and they were businessmen who owned their own land. So it was me and the old man, and after he ordered us a round of beers I put a fresh cassette in my tape recorder, set it on the table between us. I pushed the record button and this is the story that he told me:

"I was born and lived most of my young life in a pueblo called alefa, this just happened to be the place where The Immovable Object was also from. He had earned this name because he was so calm in battle, so infallible that facing off with him was like staring at a mountain side. No one had ever come close to beating him. However, the name was also indicative of his personality. He was oblivious to the world and always had been, as a boy he was not interested in futbol or beisbol like the other boys his age. He was a poor student and never ever learned to read or write. He was a poor worker, as well, prone to sleeping on the job and unresponsive to the advice and demands of his elders. Even women had no effect on him. He ignored the looks of pretty girls as he ignored everything else in the world. He lived his whole life as if he were asleep. It wasn't even until a man from the village who handled lookers recruited him that he became something other than a cause for shame and embarrassment in his town, although he did not care what people thought of him. After he became famous, still he did not care, he acted no different than he ever had, always keeping to himself, speaking rarely, and then little.

"The Immovable Object first became famous for defeating the legendary looker,

Atrius, in one of the greatest matches in the history of mirando del alma. Atrius was said to have a pure black soul, the embodiment of evil itself. It was rumored that if you locked eyes with Atrius he could steal your soul right out of your heart, or reduce it to ashes leaving you an empty shell. Many lookers would not take the table against him. But when he came looking for The Immovable Object, and challenged him to a contest, The Immovable Object accepted without even batting an eyelash, there was no fear in him.

"It was a great sight to see, the two lookers facing each other across the table. Atrius was grizzled and dirty, he was very muscular and had many knife scars on his face and arms. The Immovable Object, in contrast, looked like a child; small and soft with an unknowing face. But when they locked eyes, it was a sight to behold. For several minutes neither looker moved, they were like two wooden statues facing each other. You have never felt the kind of tension that was in this room, everyone was silent and still, barely breathing, as if time itself had come to a stop. Everyone's eyes were pouring over the lookers, waiting for some sign of weakness from one of the warriors. Then after almost four minutes, the longest contest anyone, even the old people of the village, could remember, someone spotted sweat on the forehead of Atrius, and he shouted it out to the crowd, which erupted from all the tension. Then the screaming and the yells of the spectators grew to a deafening pitch as they cheered on The Immovable Object. Atrius began to tremble and twitch like a man dying from lack of oxygen, and still the Immovable Object sat still and calm. Everyone there could see that although in their bodies Atrius was a beast, and The Immovable Object, only a boy, in their hearts the dark soul of Atrius was nothing against the will of The Immovable Object. Even though Atrius knew he was beaten he held out for as long as he could. Only after an incredible six minutes did he cry out in pain and fall to the floor covering his burning eyes. People said, even after the match was over, The Immovable Object didn't blink for several seconds. The story of this match spread throughout the south and The Immovable Object became a living legend.

"Not very long after this, word began to arrive about a looker who had an incredible record, something like 100 wins with no defeats. At first people thought it was just a legend passed from town to town by roving gamblers and unemployed fight promoters and the like. Nobody gave it very much thought. But then the rumors began to be verified by handlers and other lookers who had heard about this looker called The Unstoppable Force from people who had actually seen him. It was said that no one knew what he looked like or what his name was, and no one had ever lasted more than thirty seconds against him. Some people said he was a hypnotist, or a witch, other stories said that it was actually a woman who was so beautiful to gaze upon her would beguile any man. No matter how fantastic the story, however, everyone from the town agreed that he could never move The Immovable Object.

"When The Immovable Object was asked about these stories of the unstoppable looker he would only shrug as if there were nothing he could care less about. But the hype only got bigger, and the rumors more unbelievable until at last a confirmed match in a town about 60 miles south was to take place involving The Unstoppable Force himself. Everyone from town made the trip down to see this looker for themselves. The place where the contest was to be held was full and those who had arrived late were unable to get in. The Unstoppable Force was led into the ring by his handlers, dressed all in a black, his face bent to the floor, and covered with a hood, looking like the angel of death itself. He sat silent, with bowed head across from his opponent, a stoic looking young man with a tattoo of a spider web under his left eye. The Unstoppable Force dropped his hood, letting a mane of long dark black hair flow down his shoulders. The lookers locked eyes and when the judge said "Mirada!"the match ended. The whistle was blown, The Unstoppable Force went back under his hood and was escorted from the ring amid the shouts of angry fans who wanted their money back. No one knew what happened exactly. The judge said, simply, that the looker had broken eye contact. The loser wasn't talking, and left town that night. People who saw him said he seemed dazed, reduced to a smiling idiot, others believed he was murdered by angry men who had lost money on the match. Many people thought the match was fixed, that the loser was a hired dupe, that The Unstoppable Force was a scam, someone the odds makers had conjured up to rig matches and cash in. And where was The Unstoppable Force? No one ever saw him, knew his name or what he looked like. His handlers guarded him closely, conceding only that his mystery was part of his dominance, it was an intimidation tactic and all of the talk only added to his aura. Most of his opponents, like the kid that was beaten that night, had lost their matches before they ever took the table against him, already believing themselves that he was an unstoppable force.

"The Immovable Object had not traveled to see the contest, and knew nothing of the hysteria that had gripped the area, an hysteria that centered around him. The Immovable Object's handler was at the match, and late that evening he and The Unstoppable Force's handler brokered a deal for a match between the two legends, scheduled for two weeks from that night in the hometown of The Immovable Object, my own hometown.

"Early the next morning every small town within two hundred miles was abuzz with word of the showdown. This was to be the biggest thing that had ever happened to the small town. In the weeks before the event, the town was full of strangers, the hype produced a carnival atmosphere. The Unstoppable Force was kept under tight wraps, his whereabouts unknown, as the rumors that always hovered about him only became worse. The Immovable Object stayed mostly at home and took siestas, he seemed barely to notice all of the activity swirling around him. The handler of The Immovable Object promised the people that there would be no funny business. This was to be an honest match, and the winner would be the greatest looker of all time.

"The contest was held outdoors in order to accommodate all of the people. There was electricity in the air. It was custom for the challenger to come to the table ahead of the champion, but in this case, both lookers were champions in their own right. The handler for The Immovable Object was in a rage that the camp for The Unstoppable Force wouldn't go out first. After all, the match was in The Immovable Object's backyard. But The Unstoppable Force had over a hundred victories, to The Immovable Object's twenty-some. The matter threatened to delay the match inevitably until The Immovable Object was made aware of the situation, and entered the arena, not seeing the business in a bunch of posturing before the stare down even began.

"He strolled down to the table with his hands in his pockets to great applause, nodding politely and saying hello to folks he knew. He took his seat at the table and sat with an uninterested look on his face, waiting for The Unstoppable Force to arrive and the stare down to begin. Then the lights became dim, an organ, brought in specially, played deep tones, the crowd stirred and from out of the shadows emerged The Unstoppable Force dressed in black, surrounded by his crew, also all in black. It was a fear inspiring sight and the emotion could be felt in the room. Eyes became wide, and mouths dry. People had to fight off the urge to flee, but The Immovable Object only sat at the table watching as if he were watching a man walk down the main street on a Sunday afternoon.

"The Unstoppable Force came to the table, his face cast down, hood over his head piously. The Immovable Object glanced at him with indifference. The crowd began to murmur as The Unstoppable Force took his seat at the table across from The Immovable Object.

"The master of ceremonies read the build-up, and announced the lookers, their records, their handlers and the judges. He left the table and the judges took their places, one behind each looker, one in the middle, rotating every thirty seconds. The middle judge put his open hand in the middle.

"'Lookers, lock eyes!" he yelled, and the murmur from the crowd built to a hum. The Immovable Object, looking casually at the Unstoppable Force all the while didn't flinch, but simply located the eyes of The Unstoppable Force as he dropped his black hood revealing a head of long pitch black hair. The Unstoppable Force raised his face and cast his eyes on those of The Immovable Object.

"'Mirada!' shouted the judge as his hand shot out from between their gaze. At that first instant everyone believed that The Unstoppable Force had met his match as The Immovable Object sat staring back catatonically the way they'd seen him before, so unimpressive, so immovable.

Then the whistle blew, and the match was ended. The Immovable Object, shocked at hearing the whistle looked around to find himself sitting on the floor, his tipped-over chair beside him, surrounded by many hundred pairs of disbelieving eyes in a moving silence, as the silhouette of The Unstoppable Force and his handlers disappeared out of the door they'd come in.

"After this The Immovable Object became the subject of scorn and taunting from the people. Only now, unlike before, the words of these people wounded him deeply. Looking into the eyes of The Unstoppable Force had changed him. The Immovable Object had been moved."

The old man smiled and winked at me as he finished his second beer in a long gulp. I asked him what happened to The Immovable Object after this.

"Eventually he left Alefa and never returned, partly out of shame, but for another reason too. When The Immovable Object looked into the eyes of The Unstoppable Force he became aware, not just of his opponent and the people around him, or his little town, but of everything in the universe, of all space and time and so no longer was he content to work as a farmhand in his tiny village. In fact, I hear he is still alive, walking the roads of the world, looking at life, and engaging with people, occasionally telling them a good story for the price of a couple of beers."

As the old man rose from his chair to leave, I asked him if The Immovable Object ever described what it was about the eyes of The Unstoppable Force that was so powerful. The old man sighed and looked up at nothing as he tried to think of the right word. "The eyes of The Unstoppable Force were like ... Truth," he said.

I asked him how he knew this, if The Immovable Object had told him so, or if he had just heard it. He clapped me hard on the shoulder and looked down at me with gentle old eyes. "Take my word for it," he said through a smile of crooked brown teeth. Then he winked, and walked out of the tavern leaving me to pay for his beer.

Spring Ulmer

Jumah

■ ■ ■

You've attempted suicide twelve times, and now you're on another hunger strike. Strapped into a restraint chair, a feeding tube forced up your nose, down your throat, and into your stomach, you scream. Officials at Guantánamo pump you full of liquid nutrients and laxatives and keep you in the chair until you shit yourself.

An African-American soldier tells you he is sorry. You thank him. He doesn't want your thanks. He wants you to know we're not all bad, and we think differently. Another soldier cries. *These are examples,* you write on a piece of paper that your lawyer smuggles out of Guantánamo, *to show the reader that there are some soldiers who have humanity, irrespective of their race, gender or faith.*

■

What Thou Lovest Well Remains American — I can't get this poem by Richard Hugo out of my head. The poem indicts America for degrading a person beyond repair, while lovingly rendering the emptiness of a nameless small town in North America. I imagine the town in the poem is Denison, Iowa — home of Tom Hogan, maker of the restraint chair in which you have been strapped. I ask the woman behind the desk at the Budget Inn if there is anything happening in Denison. She has long, fake, pink fingernails and dandruff on her face. *Not that I know of,* she says, handing me a key. It is unusually cold for September. I'm shivering in my thin *Shut Down Guantánamo* T-shirt. *Guantánamo* from the Spanish *aguantar*, meaning to bear no more.

I sleep in my clothes, wake at eight, and check out of my room. What kind of place and person manufactures the restraint chair? I breakfast at the Trio Café across from Landscapes Unlimited cement lawn ornament store on Denison's main drag, Lincoln Highway. Before entering the café, I feed quarters into the newspaper dispenser. I jiggle the handle, but it won't open. Two older women watch me through the window. I give up and push open the café door. Before me a flier reads: *25 Clay Birds $3.00 Shooting Club Wednesdays,* and inside the café walls are decorated with paintings of animals with guns. The women at the booth by the window tell me there are papers at the counter. On the front page of the *Souix City Journal* is a photo of Iraqis burning an effigy of the Pope. I order an English muffin and coffee.

Everyone here knows each other — it's obvious by the way they talk and joke. I pretend to read the paper, but really I am eavesdropping. At one table, a woman talks about her mother, *I tried her cell phone and she ain't answering. She's got half-timers — forgets half of what you tell her.* The other talk is of cutting hay, the price of houses, and of living in the country where you don't have to see your neighbors.

The first person I say more than a few words to in Denison is dressed in a blue vest. I meet her at Thrifty White, a drug store in the city center. *No, we don't stock film,* she apologizes. *It expires before we can sell it and everyone shoots digital these days.* She has shockingly blue eyes and her white hair is cut short. I ask if she's lived here long. *Forty-two years.* She tells me she moved here to bury her first husband.

What's the biggest thing that's changed? I ask.

The biggest change in Denison? The Hispanics, she says. *I'm not saying it's a bad change. They carry a lot more things at the grocery they didn't carry then.*

I've read of Denison's segregation, and I know of the blossoming hate in this country when it comes to issues of immigration. I ask her, then, about Tom Hogan — wording what I say carefully, so it doesn't sound like I'm on one side or the other. *He's a super guy,* she says, smiling. *Someone told me he was a general in the military! Heard him on the radio this morning talking about the storm. Have you been out to his house and seen his chairs? I used to lived next door to him. He should be at the sheriff's office now. I'm sure he'll talk to you....*

I exit Thrifty White and walk down Broadway, the sidewalk lined with brick-boxed cement casts of children's handprints. Stepping around the construction site with its Spanish-speaking workers and wooden billboard announcing the birth of a new jail, I approach the police station. A large young man eating junk food on the other side of the station's Plexiglas window buzzes me in. I climb the stairs and answer a thin woman's what do you want? Minutes later, after staring at the painting of a yellow-eyed owl on the wall, I'm shaking hands with Tom Hogan.

Jumah, I think the reason I'm telling you this is the same reason I keep writing you letters that keep getting returned, some ripped open, others unread, all of the envelopes stamped "Refused." It's because not writing would imply giving up, would imply thinking writing doesn't matter, and Jumah, I can't think this. But one can hang only so much on one line before it begins to droop — and a boat when it tips begins to fill — so think of my letters to you as buckets, bailing against the waves that are swallowing you up.

■

A mentally ill person said it should have padding and be painted blue, so we changed it, Tom Hogan tells me. He's taken me to the basement to show me the chair. *She said, 'I didn't think you would listen to me because I'm mentally ill,' but I told her, 'I think you're the person we should be listening to.'* The chair sits by itself against a block wall, looking like a weight-lifting bench that's been bent in half. Hogan removes the warning that is rubber-banded to the chair handle, and reads it to me, underlining each word with his finger.

Anytime you restrain someone there's a risk, he explains after reattaching the warning to the chair. Then he lists examples. When he gets to the hog tie, he acts it out for me. *It's where you cuff the arms and then tuck the legs behind them like this. The hog tie can asphyxiate. So we made the chair.*

We? I ask.

My wife and I. Then the hospitals wanted it. I said okay, I could see the need. Then the military wanted it.

I interrupt to ask him how he feels about 25 of his chairs ending up at Guantánamo.

I deplore torture. I think any time you demean or humiliate someone that's torture and I think we should uphold the Geneva Conventions, every single one. As soon as you say you can waterboard, it's a slippery slope. But I'm not sure how my chair's being used —

Are you going to continue to sell it? I ask.

He doesn't answer.

Instead he says, *Commandant Hood at Guantánamo called me the other day and said, 'I bet you never got a call from Cuba before.' Then he told me, 'I just want to let you know we're not torturing anybody down here.' That made me feel better, I slept better that night.*

Let me put it another way, I say. *If you knew absolutely the chair was being used to torture, would you stop selling it?*

I'd like to believe I am good. We all have good and bad in us. You never know.

■

The restraint chair breaks your hunger strike, Jumah. You aren't near death. They don't force feed you to save you, even though Tom Hogan says he designed the chair to help save lives. The time now is 9:48 a.m. The day: November 19. Two months have passed since I last wrote to you. I sit at my desk in Iowa City, and study the photograph taken of you before you were detained. You are dressed in a blue sweater and hold a pencil next your mouth as you talk on the phone. I study your ruffled brown hair and averted eyes and imagine smoking cigarettes with you in a garden and talking about books. I'm not sure why I feel close to you, close enough to write letters, to imagine a correspondence. Perhaps, initially, it was seeing this photo — in which you seem so like myself — not because you are on the phone, but because this photograph portrays a recognizable need you have to communicate.

As I write, I am continually reminded of the fact my freedom of speech, in some manner, be it symbolic or literal, costs you your freedom. I am also aware that my ability to enjoy the light of the morning as it penetrates the slightly see-through white cloth covering my window is dependent on your solitary confinement, your being held, cuffed to a dungeon filled with chemical odors and loud music.

I have read your prison narrative; I have read, *As I hold my pen, my hand is shaking;* I have read of your being urinated on, made to walk barefoot on barbed wire, stripped of clothes and left naked with no pillow, no mattress, only the cold metal of the cage. I have read of the petrol injected into your penis, of your slit throat, of the time your lawyer came and you excused yourself, made a noose and jumped from the sink in the bathroom.

No one should be shackled to the ground and menstruated on. No one, Jumah.

How, in the face of this, can I write to you? And of what can I write? Of the color of the sweater I am wearing — pale-green?

Adam Hahn

Leave This Thermostat at Seventy-two Degrees

■ ■ ■

(JAKE sits at a table with a peach and a knife. SARAH is carrying in groceries. She's going over a mental list of things she needs to tell JAKE.)

SARAH
Leave this thermostat at seventy-two degrees.

JAKE
That's kind of cold.

SARAH
I like it cold.

JAKE
Isn't that too cold at night?

SARAH
If you need an extra blanket, they're in the cedar chest.

JAKE
Couldn't we turn the AC off at night and not need extra blankets?

SARAH
I like it cold when I get up in the morning.

JAKE
Seventy-two is really cold.

SARAH
Wear long sleeves. In the winter, I set the thermostat at sixty, but you don't have to worry about that, except you'll probably want to wear sweaters.

Food. I keep a list on the counter of things I need as I run out of them. You can add to the list, or if you go shopping take the list with you. I'll try to be specific. I'm really particular about brands —

JAKE
I know you are —

SARAH
— so please do read the list. If they're out of the brand I wrote down, just don't bother. I'd rather wait and pick it up the next time.

Produce. Maybe it's better if I buy the produce.

JAKE
I'm not allowed to buy produce?

SARAH
You're allowed. I'm just kind of picky about produce. Fruit, anyway. I know what I like, and I don't buy fruit unless it's perfect. You can buy fruit, but that'll just be for you.

JAKE
If I buy fruit, you won't eat it?

SARAH
Probably not.

JAKE
You've eaten fruit I bought before.

SARAH
That was different. It was in your kitchen.

I didn't have a choice.

I was going to make a list of where everything goes in the kitchen, but you've been over enough I think it'll be easier if we just deal with things as they come up. If you don't know where something goes, ask. If I'm not home, just leave it on the counter, or put the whole bag of groceries in the refrigerator.

JAKE
I know how to put away groceries.

SARAH
It's a new kitchen for you, and I've had time to work out a system so everything goes somewhere.

JAKE
It's not that big a deal if I put the peanut butter on the wrong shelf.

SARAH
I don't buy peanut butter.

JAKE
I do.

SARAH
I never buy peanut butter. The entire time I've lived here —

If you feel the need to buy peanut butter, then I'll make room for it. For now, just leave it on the counter. I'll figure out where it goes.

Laundry. If you want me to wash your clothes, I will. Just leave everything in the hamper. Don't bother sorting.

If you think you'll want to do laundry, we need to talk about the washer and dryer. I don't like to waste water —

JAKE
I know how to do laundry.

SARAH
Please don't wash the sheets.

JAKE
What?

SARAH
I don't like using too much fabric softener on the sheets, but they generate a lot of static. I have —

JAKE
You have a system.

SARAH
Right.

JAKE
Sarah, look at me.

Am I moving in because we love each other and we want to live together, or because we're both broke and you can't afford the rent here alone?

(long pause)

JAKE (CONT'D)
If I'm just a roommate, we can buy separate groceries.

SARAH
You're not just a roommate.

JAKE
I don't want to mess up your system. Could you set aside part of the refrigerator for my food? Could I have one cupboard for my peanut butter?

SARAH
I love you.

You're moving in because we're broke. We both knew that. If you could afford to stay in your place, you wouldn't be here.

That doesn't mean we don't love each other.

I could have found a roommate. I have that spare room. I'd rather live with you.

(JAKE cuts the peach.)

JAKE
I bought peaches today. They're fantastic.

Try one.

(SARAH takes a small piece. She eats it very slowly.)

JAKE (CONT'D)
Have more.

SARAH
That peach is bruised.

(THE END)

Nick Compton

Redhorse Revelry

∎ ∎ ∎

All is beautiful, the spring is well. Fresh air, strong current, live bait. Try to stop me.

Those days were glorious. The river crawled slowly, ink-black and powerful. It was flowing calligraphy in an ancient valley. Towering oaks and sprawling willow trees lined the upper-bank, their sagging branches gently sipping the water. Below, nearer the shore, brittle reeds whistled in the wind, laughing at the fisherman who would come and crunch them.

I was young then, and my father was old. We'd scale down the riverbank like shadows in the fading sun. Discreet and calculated, because the fish are intelligent, my dad would say. Noise is disrespectful. The incline was steep and oftentimes muddy from the frequent spring downpours, but the river cast an entrancing spell, too powerful to ignore. We'd settle in and he'd prepare the rods, my father. Tight knots, fresh bait, and sharp hooks. He was the best surgeon I'd ever seen. He was careful with the tackle, cupping sinkers, chartreuse-colored beads, and treble hooks like a mother cradles a first-born. We'd sit on buckets rigged dangerously into the hillside, unbalanced and uncomfortable. The sun would be shining, then, and the spring air exploding with life. Robins danced around us, singing in glorious cadence, and insects, as vast and varied as the universe, emerged from the winter's dullness. He'd cast for me. Low, strong and confident. I wasn't sure where he was aiming, but I was certain he never missed the mark. When both lines were cast, I'd sometimes venture into the hillside, finding forked-sticks to stab into the earth and perch our rods on. Other times, we held them ourselves, keeping a finger on the line, feeling the soft kiss of the bottom flirt with our fingertips. Dad preferred this.

I'd study the river, then, marvel at its impenetrable darkness. The power of its current steady against the stable riverbank. I watched logs and other snags flow by, on a journey I couldn't fathom. He'd point, my father, to my rod tip hoisted high in the air. Tap, tap … tap,tap … tap-tap-tap, a short, biting rhythm that plays in my dreams. I'd nod and grab the reel, my finger-tip diagnosing the line. He'd taught me to see with the nerves of my fingers. Concentration was essential, I closed my eyes and felt. Felt as she played with the bait, knocking into it stupidly.

I felt when the hook pierced her mouth, and felt when she darted away into darkness, afraid and attached to a line. My father also taught me to set the hook, not hard, but not soft. He taught me to reel, not fast yet not too slow. And he taught me to fight the catch, respecting the ancient challenge. They were strong, the redhorse we sought, and they feared the daylight with every cell in their body. They were curious creatures, traversing this river only once a year to lay their eggs and perpetuate the rhythm of life. The females were hugely pregnant, bursting with eggs. The males were virile and eager, spilling sperm on the touch.

A paradox when they broke the surface, their large fins wine-red and thrusting against the licorice-black water. Their scales were smooth and their mouths shaped into a comical pucker. He taught me to get them on shore, quickly, without letting them flop about. He showed me how to snatch them in one quick movement and remove the hook from their mouths. He'd throw the fish back immediately, he looked mad when they bled and even madder when they surfaced twenty feet downstream, like they sometimes did. If the hook was clean, he'd pick a fresh worm to impale. If the worm was reusable, there was no need to change. Then he'd cast, low and strong, into that mysterious life-force — never far from where the sinker splashed before. And with this, not a word, there was never a need and I could never find one. Not to suffice. It was beautiful, just beautiful.

Rick Zollo

Requiem for Jim's Rig

He rode his silver chariot, Mitsubishi Mirage, cross-town in traffic
Years of caution made him light on the pedal, but don't press him
He's dangerous, pregnant with thought; his measure exceeds his shadow
And his gentleness belies strong conviction

He did not drive cars that spoke of manhood in horsepower
He did not care for show and tell, prowess over what was under the hood
He wanted quality and value and utility, please
He was a man who knew his worth and cared little about appearance

Still, in early years he drove fearlessly, once riding an old beater up
From Baltimore to New Haven, brake linings worn out so that he
Slowed the stead through double pumps and prayers to lost Gods
Foot dragging on pavement (car's floor rusted away) to get the rig to stop

Now no longer fearless, he took another tack and lived
By a creek near the old trolley storage yard on the East Side
Took to wandering the city slowly, pondering lost youth and new age
Philosophies as he made his fateful journey into middle age

Sage teacher, he bought the Silver Mirage and it served him well
Many years his loyal conveyance as he trekked about town
And when the car lost a bumper, he replaced it with another
White against silver, the chariot's two-tone color a contrast he endured

Now the late great Mirage sits curbside, retired from travel, replaced by a
Dark blue Volvo with a sunroof he will never use
The man eschews show and still drives soft on the pedal, wisdom advising
Slow go through city streets. Message: caution! Man at work.

Peter Feldstein
2537
Ink Jet Print from digital drawing (Adobe Illustrator)

Barry Sharp
Arcadia Schooner
Digital Photograph, 16" x 20", Camera: Nikon D100

Andrew Whitters
Broken Bottles
Hand constructed stoneware clay that is buffed by hand, with a white crackle glaze
Red bottle — 2', 2" tall with base diameter of 5"
Blue bottle — 9" tall with a base diameter of 4"
Purple bottle (with "J" engraved) — 1', 11" tall with a base diameter of 5"
Brown bottle — 9" tall with a base diameter of 3"

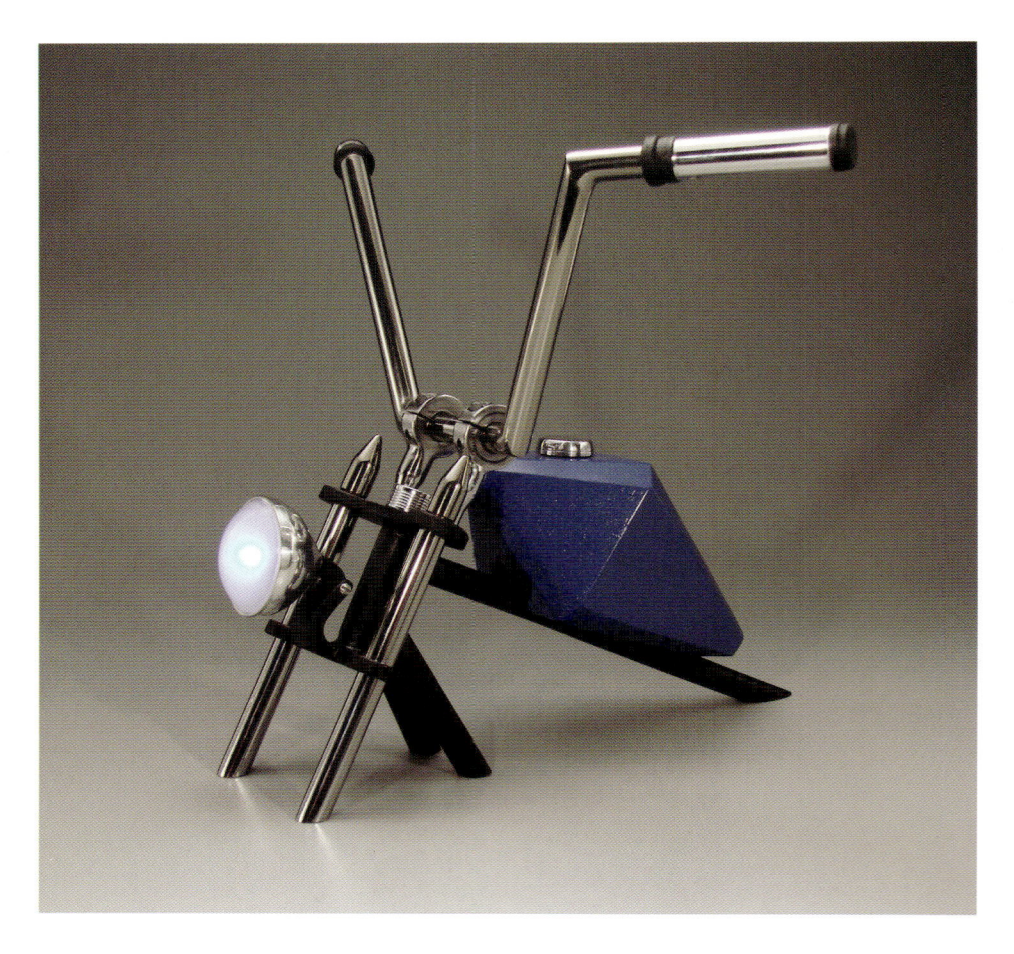

Jason Messier
Chopper Teapot
Steel, aluminum, plexiglass, brass, powder-coat, 12" x 12" x 12"

Marcia Wegman
Early Spring
Dry pastel, 28" x 24"

Kenn Hubel
Blossoms, Tree, Oregon Coast
Digital photograph, 10" x 15"

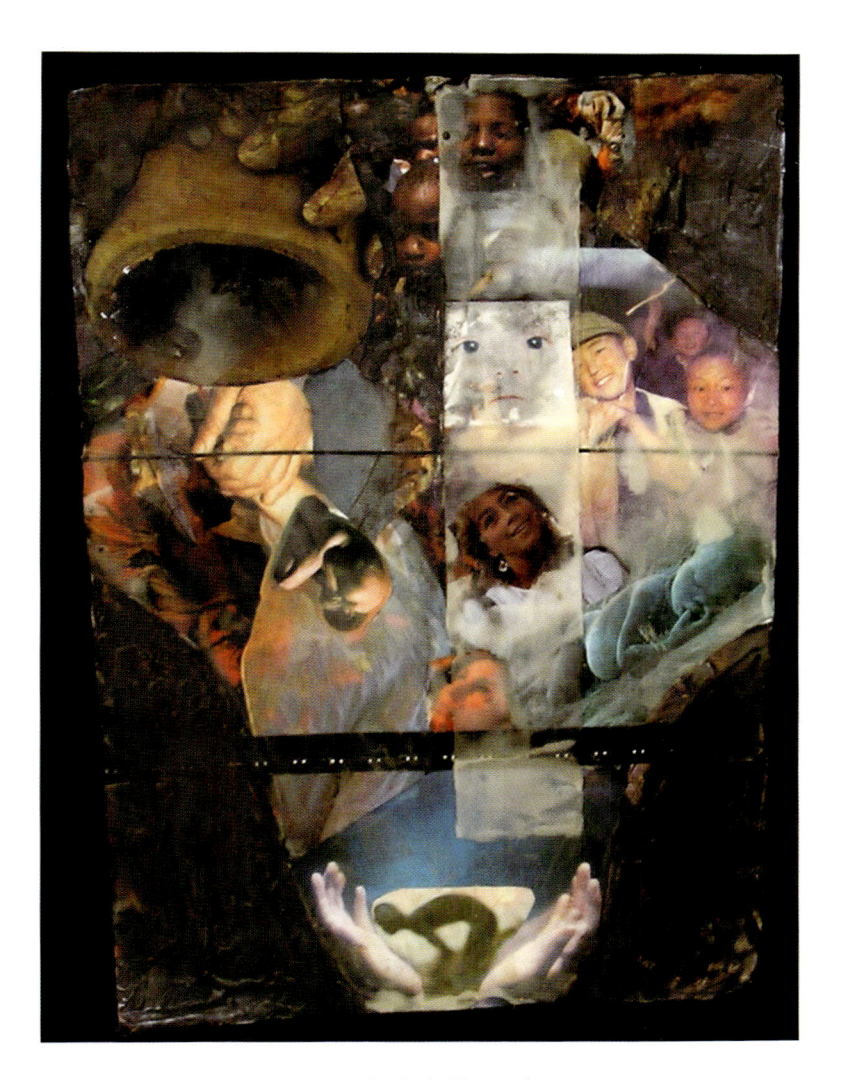

Rita Svoboda Tomanek
Body of Christ, Save Me
Encaustic collage, 21" x 33" framed

Laura Young
Ascent
Oil, acrylic, pencil, on paper, 30" x 22"

Craig Albright
Field
Oil on panel, 25" x 32"

Matt Lyvers
Changes
Pastel on Bristol, 57" x 24"

Jan Krieger
Emma and Harley
Gelatin silver print, 10" x 10"

Ramon Lim
Dance
Chinese calligraphy, ink on paper

Dale Phillips
Glowing Trumpet
Photograph, Canon S5IS digital, 13" x 19"

Patricia Knox
New Elation 2
Reticulation silver, sterling silver, copper, 14K gold, moss agate,
$2^{1}/_{4}$" x $2^{1}/_{2}$" x $^{3}/_{4}$"

Brittany Noethen
Musical Truth
From the altered book "Rhythm"

Mixed media: collage and image transfer on acrylic paint, 9" x 11"

Cheryl Jacobsen
Only Echoes
Watercolor, gouache and graphite on calfskin vellum, 11" x 9"
Text by Stuart Davis

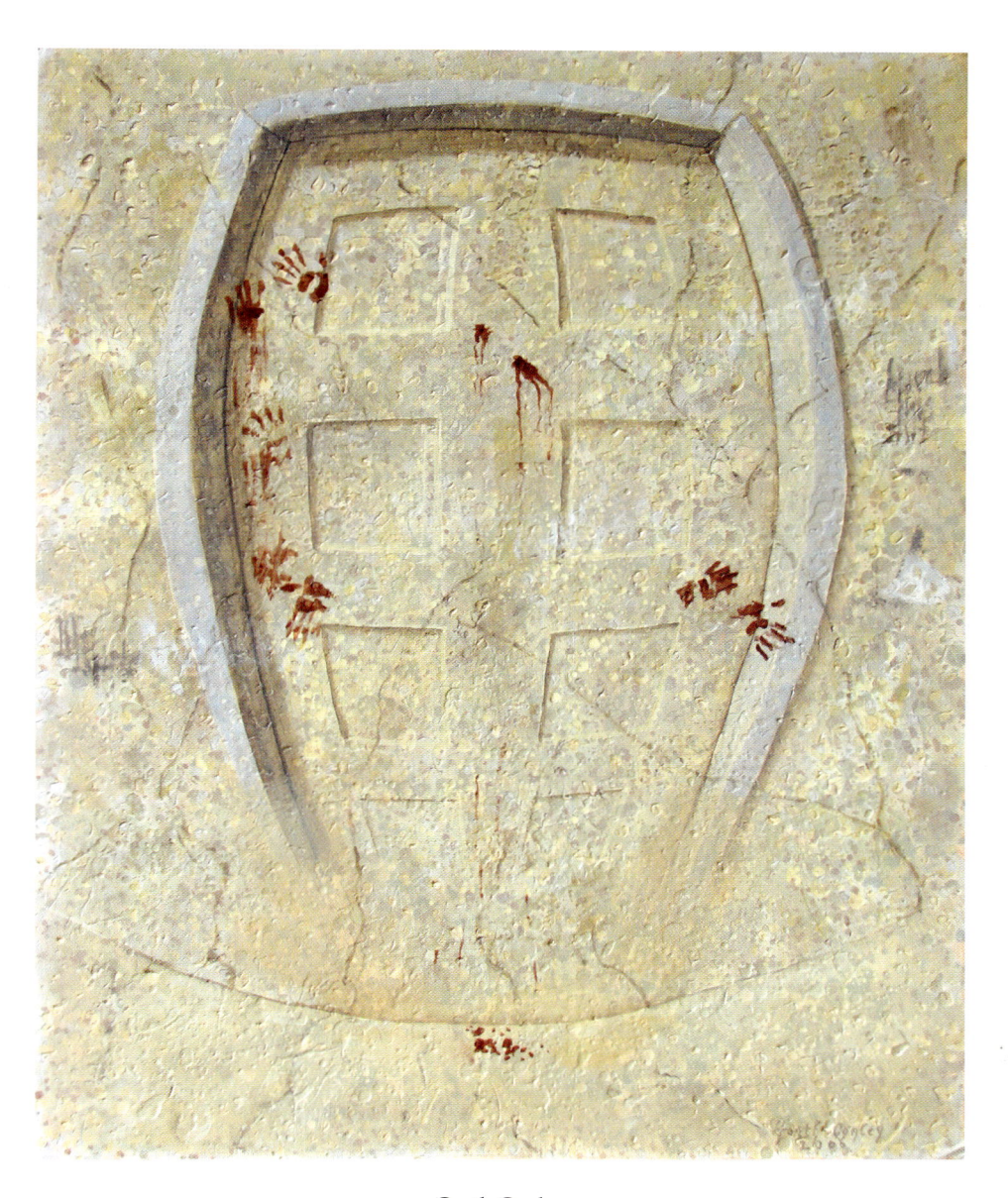

Garth Conley
Dreams Done: Looking Ahead
Oil on canvas panel, 20" x 16"

Connie Roberts
Rub A Dub Dub
Carved wood with acrylic paint; the heads are removable whistles

10" x 10" X 12"

Gordon Kellenberger
Eastern Iowa Landscape
Pastel, 20" x 26"

Tom Aprile
Domestic Extrusions
Oil on paper with collage, 29" x 41"

Elizabeth Roberts
Anxiety
Figure is wax, synthetic hair, synthetic eyelashes, human hair, acrylic paint; base is wood, acrylic paint, 20" x 16" x 9"

Shirley Wyrick
Free Flow
Installation: 4' x 4.3' x 8.3'
Bronze elements: 49"

Sophie Radl
Walking Back
Photograph, 5" x 7"

Astrid Hilger Bennett
Balances
Artquilt using fabrics handpainted and monoprinted by the artist, 48" x 66"

Paul Cork
Tiamah 08
Watercolor, 2.9"' x 4.5"

Linda & Robert Scarth
Iowa River Sunset
Photograph, 16" x 20"

Bernice Gantz
Les Fleur
Watercolor, 19" x 21"

Zakery Neumann
Early Evening Sun
Photograph, 11" x 14"

Tonya Kehoe
California
Acrylic and mixed media on wooden panel, 18" x 30"

Jason Strating
One
Acrylic, 24" x 24"

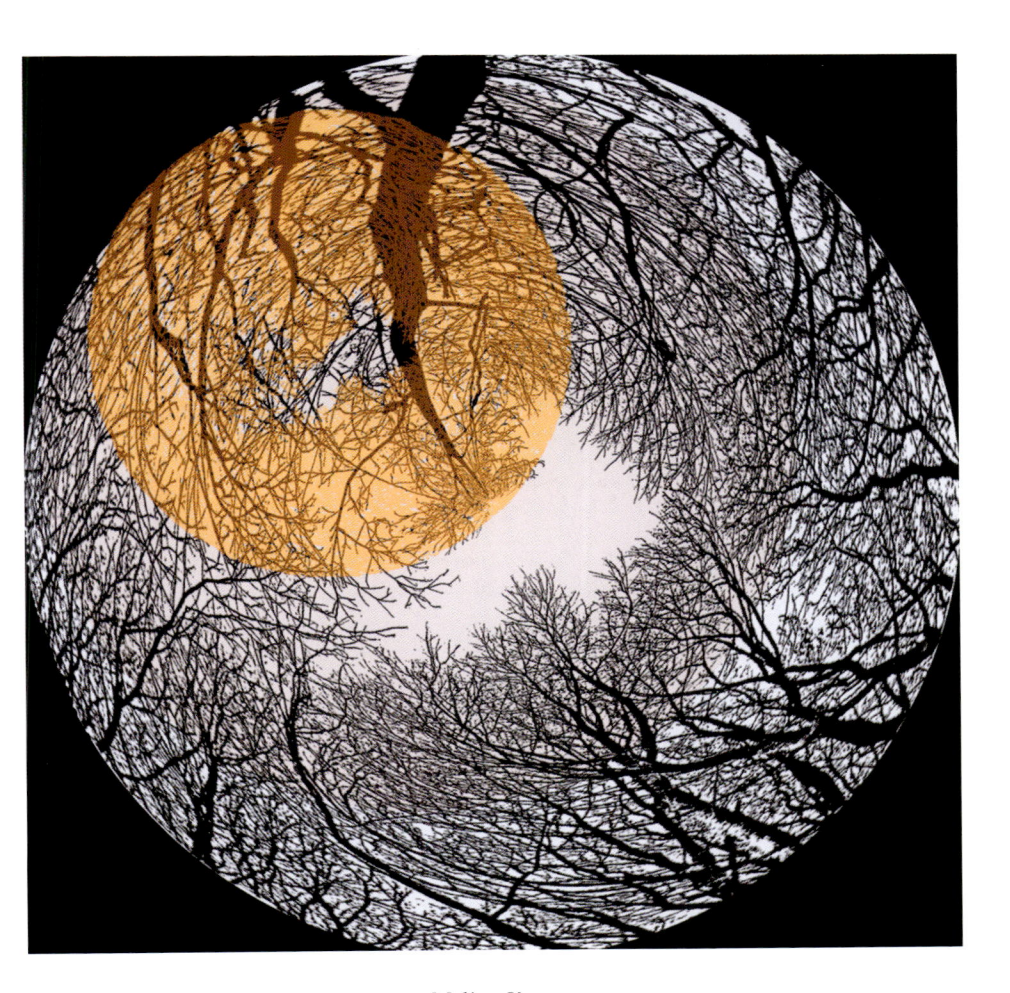

Melina Kaune
Treesphere
Digital manipulation photo collage, 10" x 10"

Mindy Stukel
Riding the Rails
Shot with a Canon EOS Rebel 2K SLR camera using Ilford's HP 400 black and white film, 8" x 10"

The Bomb Shaman
God & Chaos
Acrylic, 9" x 12"

Nick Meister
Sherbert Posers
Watercolor, 22" x 30"

Julie Fitzpatrick
Slim to None
Acrylic on canvas, 10" x 30"

Howard Cox
Suspended DewDrops
Color photograph, Canon 20D

Jeff McNutt
All Aboard Herky
Oil and Kinnick Stadium brick dust on canvas, 36" x 38"

Phyllis Lance
Dragonfly
Watercolor, 9" x 11"

Howard Hinton Jr.
Water Works
Photograph, Canon 20D

Sue Hershberger
Early Morning Mist
Photograph, 5" x 7"

Mary Carson

Tree

I have a photo of my son
climbing in the unscreened kitchen window up a little tree,
a volunteer, a mulberry, that slanted toward the house.
I didn't have the will, or sense, to cut it down.
He was 8, with long pale hair that curled a little as does mine.
His face was radiant with the climbing feat and summer and our country house
and his new life.
The sapling grew into a tree.
I hung an end of clothesline on it and a metal pan
to feed the birds.
A hive of bees settled in it once,
clustered on their queen, moved on.
The long limb with the feeder stretched across the window tirelessly,
giving its green to the room, calming it in verdant shadow
from the fierceness of the western sun.
A baby came, and then another, children of my child.
I have some footage of this second baby on the kitchen table, fat and cooing,
watching out the window
at the light play off its leaves.
We had to dig the septic up one summer, for a root had broken in to get a drink.
Woe to thirsty trees.
I cut it way back with my saw.
The rest of it died the next few years, and
so it was a big dead trunk with one dead limb.
Still I hung my clothesline, fed my birds.
I put what was left of it into the stove today, chunks of rotting wood,
like pocked brown pieces of the moon.
They came to be while we were
growing up and old. The same time is marked
within their cells, caught in some blessed way.
And there they go, finally, warming up my winter walls,
giving their captured sun life to this instant of mine,
asking for nothing.

Helen Thompson

The Cost of Freedom

■ ■ ■

Our eyes are closed. We lie six feet apart, and we are silent. The sun never shines when we are together, and sometimes the sunless sky and the silence are overwhelming. Those days, the salt dries my skin, and I make a mental note to use moisturizer when I get home. The absurdity of contemplating Oil of Olay at a time like this sends me into maniacal fits of giggles and heartbreak, and it reminds me that she was my sanity. I miss her.

■

We were 13 when Sarah taught me how to make oatmeal the good way.

"That is NOT how you make oatmeal!" she laughed as I poured cold water over Quaker Peaches and Cream and headed for the microwave. I watched her heat up water and pour tiny streams into her bowl until she had a thick lumpy mound of oatmeal. Sarah held out a spoonful, and it was in my mouth before I could protest.

"THAT is how you make oatmeal."

I haven't been able to touch the runny concoction my mother made since. Sarah challenged my conventional methods of everything. She was six days older and infinitely wiser. Shoes were shackles, and if she went anywhere, she went barefoot. She force-fed me liberation from the norms of our Midwest society, and one day I realized that something had shifted in the way I saw the world. My oatmeal was lumpy, and I was no longer wearing my shoes.

One spring later, she was screaming at me from 18 inches away as the wind whipped our hair and the harnesses bruised our shoulders. We were a half-second from dropping 40 feet, and we were the coaster's only and front row passengers on a gray Thursday in March.

"Helen! Open your eyes!" I peeked out one eye, and held on for dear life.

I didn't know a fear like that again until a year later, when she held my hand and told me it was a boy. And nearly two years after that, when she told me it was a girl.

My daughter's father was crazy sometimes, and Sarah would come over and rescue the kids and I until he ran out of methamphetamine and crashed for 36 hours on the living room floor. He would scream and throw empty pop cans at her car as we drove away.

Once, we came back a day too early, and cigarette burned photographs and bloody razorblades littered the bathroom floor. He was nowhere in sight, and we took the razors and left again, hoping the next time to choose our arrival date more carefully. Sarah looked at me, all soft green eyes and auburn hair made of satin. "You know this isn't love," she smiled sadly. "This is wrong, and love doesn't feel like this."

Her words fell on self-deafened ears. I trapped myself in this relationship with my own guilt, and I absolved my indiscretions with his anger and abuse. I thought I'd stick around until he had hurt me just enough to cancel out the pain I had caused him, and then I could end it. I knew the relationship with him wouldn't last, but I couldn't let go of my desire to be redeemed, even for her. In my naive young mind, Sarah and I were indestructible. We had forever, and I just needed him for a little longer.

One bright sunny morning in August, my cell phone displayed a missed call from Sarah's grandmother. "That's weird." I said. He looked at me with cold eyes.

"She's probably dead."

I dialed the numbers I still knew from our childhood and stared blankly at the steering wheel as her grandmother's words passed through my conscious mind in a jumble. Car. Accident. Hospital. Passed. Away. I hung up the phone.

"She's dead," I said.

"I told you so."

I turned my head slowly to face him in the passenger seat and I realized what I had taken for granted. I stared into the eyes of every naive and wasteful decision I had ever made, and I watched those eyes make a mockery of the only real love I had ever known.

And I untied my laces, and removed my shoes.

∎

We are alone and together. We are silent under our perpetually gray sky. She is me and I am her, and neither of us are really here in this cold field of cement blocks and terminal flowers and tears. Right now, together, we only exist in the time of bare feet and freedom when we ruled the world.

Carol Blomberg

The Wise Tree and the Foolish Bush

■ ■ ■

The wise, old grandfather tree's far reaching branches blew gently in the wind as they extended out over the refreshing, gurgling stream below. The grandfather tree was looking down at a tiny, young sapling several feet away from his trunk and a small bush just beyond the sapling. As he spoke, his words were carried by the wind to the two of them.

"Young ones, I have something very important that I want to share with you. I am a very old tree and my days are not many now. I know that my branches will not bear leaves this spring and I will soon return to the dirt of the earth from where I sprung up from. Before long, I will be with you no more."

The young tree and the young bush looked up at the immense tree that towered over them. The small tree loved the grandfather tree deeply and he was the first to respond.

"Grandfather tree, please don't talk about your leaving. I can not bear it when you talk like this. Say that you will always be here with us?" pleaded the young seedling.

"If only I could, but I can not, young one. If I were to tell you so, it would not be true, my child," spoke the old grandfather tree soothingly.

The young bush chimed in impatiently, "What is it that you would tell us, old one?"

The wind rustled the leaves of the massive, old grandfather tree. "Listen to my words carefully, plant them deep in your roots. As your branches grow toward the sky and reach for the sun, let your roots extend ever deeply, always reaching for the stream. You will be wise to look to the stream for ..."

The young bush abruptly interrupted the old grandfather tree in mid-sentence.

"My roots are going to grow right near the surface of the ground so that when the rains fall upon the land, I will drink deeply. I don't want to depend on anyone and certainly not a silly old stream. Yes, I will trust only in myself," said the little bush with great confidence.

Now it was the young tree who found himself interrupting, as he told the little bush to be quiet. "Grandfather tree, I am listening, please, continue."

The grandfather tree was silent. "Grandfather!" yelled the small tree, but there was no response from the grandfather tree.

The spring season came upon the land and the spring rains poured forth from the skies in great abundance. The tears of the little tree fell in unison with the pouring rain as he mourned the passing away of the grandfather tree. There were no green leaves bursting forth from the grandfather tree's branches this season, just as he had said there would not be. The heavy rains came accompanied by high, blustery winds. Soon the brittle branches of the grandfather tree began to snap and break off, one by one, crashing loudly to the ground below.

The small bush did exactly what he said he was going to do, he grew his roots right near the ground's surface. The little tree was astounded at the rapid growth of the little bush.

That spring and the following spring the bush seemed to explode with growth as his branches grew long and full. Beautiful white flowers burst forth on his limbs and the bees swarmed from flower to flower drinking their fill of nectar. After the beautiful flowers faded, the bush was soon overflowing with luscious red berries. Year after year the bush grew and grew, its foliage thick and green. Many different kinds of birds came to feed from the bush and they built their nests and raised their young in the safety of the bush's dense boughs.

The little tree grew much, much slower than the bush, but it never forgot the last thing the grandfather tree had shared. The little tree was diligent to extend his roots deeply and always in the direction of the stream, just as the grandfather tree had instructed.

At times, however, the little tree would find himself battling with jealousy and envy as he watched in ever increasing amazement the flourishing bush, who seemed to be continually surrounded by birds, bees and other animals who were attracted to the bush's thick, green foliage.

The little tree looked at his own sparse branches, in comparison, and he counted the few pieces of fruit that dangled from his own skinny limbs. He longed to have birds and bees swarming about him as they did the bush and, often times, he found himself becoming quite dismayed and discouraged. It was at times like these that he would think to himself that maybe, he too, should grow shallow roots like the bush, but then he would be reminded of the grandfather tree's last words, and he would find himself even more determined to extend his roots deeper and ever reaching toward the stream.

Year after year the rains came, each and every spring, without exception, and every year the bush would tell the tree how foolish he was to have listened to the rantings and ravings of the old grandfather tree, who obviously in his last days had been delirious and nonsensical.

By now, all of the dead, dry limbs of the grandfather tree had fallen to the ground and only a short stump remained left of him as lightning had struck his once massive trunk and had caused the great majority of the trunk to come crashing down.

One spring season the rains did not come when they usually did. The land and the animals waited and waited, but the rains still did not come. The landscape became dry and barren and the wind mercilessly tossed and blew the sand and dirt about everywhere.

The following spring, there were still no rains. The heavens were shut up and the land found itself in the midst of a severe drought. The bush became dry and brittle and his beautiful, appealing white flowers failed to come into bloom and his branches were fruitless as they ceased to produce their luscious red berries. There were no animals seeking shelter anymore under his branches nor were any birds of the air nesting in his boughs. The land itself resembled a dry, stony wilderness.

However, in the midst of this drought, the tree, which by now had grown to be gloriously tall and stately, seemed to go untouched by the lack of rain. His far-stretching roots, ever extending over the years to the stream, had reached the stream bed and though the stream was not overflowing as it had been in seasons past when the rains were abundant, the winding stream still trickled throughout the land and watered all whose roots extended toward it.

The tree's leaves were as green and full as ever and his boughs were overladen with luscious, sweet fruit. All species of birds took refuge in the tree's ample branches, making their homes in his strong limbs and feasting on the tree's plentiful fruit. Animals from all around, seeking relief from the intense heat of the sun, came and rested in the shade of the tree's thick, firm boughs.

"O tree, I admit now my foolishness. You were right to have listened to the old grandfather tree. I see now the error of my ways," admitted the bush remorsefully.

Both the tree and the bush knew that the hour was getting late for the bush unless it was to rain soon. That very evening, a fierce windstorm descended upon the land. The mighty tree stood firm and unmoved as the winds pushed and pulled and uprooted everything that stood in its path. The tree watched, helplessly, as one particularly powerful gust of wind uprooted the bush's shallow roots violently from the ground and caused the bush to roll and roll and roll, right out of the tree's sight. The bush was gone and there was absolutely no trace of his ever having been there. The tree was overcome by sadness.

It was not until the following spring season that the long drought finally broke. The heavens opened up once again and shower after shower fell upon the land. The stream bulged at its banks again and the land was covered and enveloped in a blanket of green.

In the same spot where the previous bush had resided all those many years a small bush grew up out of the ground. The tree's heart was warmed to see the tiny bush.

The slight breeze carried the words of the tree to the young bush. "Can I share something important with you, my child?" asked the tall, stately tree.

"What would you tell me, old one?" said the young bush looking up at the immense tree that towered over him.

"Listen to my words carefully, plant them deep in your roots. As your branches grow toward the sky, and reach for the sun, let your roots extend ever deeply, always reaching for the stream. You will be wise to look to the stream for ...," the tree paused for a moment to see if the young bush was still listening and the tree was pleased to see that he was.

"Don't stop," said the small bush, "tell me more."

The wind gently rustled the leaves of the tree. The tree looked down at the young bush as he continued on, smiling as he did so.

PJM Atkinson

A Hundred Acres

A hundred acres, more or less
That's where we keep the cows
Who calve in spring and graze all year
Their hooves carving up the ground

And this is where you find the deer
nibbling sweet corn and clover
Or rubbing trees with velvet antlers
And chasing does in winter

This is where the turkeys trot
Snapping grasshoppers from the hay
Streaming poults or dragging beards
And strutting for a mate

This is where the wood ducks fly
And circle to the creek
Last year they had a little nest
But didn't have any offspring

And here is where the coyotes cry
And prowl for their next meal
Gray or black or motley brown
They prefer not to reveal

And here the foxes yip, yip, yip
And scour every slough
Hoping for a tasty mouse
Though sometimes bugs will do

This is where the raccoons romp
And eat from mulberry trees
They fish with little sharp-clawed hands
Sifting through the reeds

A hundred acres, more or less
That's where I belong
My soul will linger in those woods
Long after I am gone.

Lois Muehl

Shopping with Zorro — Iowa City '58

Looking neither right nor left, holding his head stiffly proud beneath the flat-brimmed vaquero hat, the graceful figure in the swirling cape strode through the Saturday mob.

Behind the black mask dark eyes glittered. Beneath it, an unmistakable mustache twitched. No one who passed glanced at his woman companion. All eyes fixed on the fearless warrior in disguise, attacker of the unjust, protector of the poor.

"Hi, Zorro!"

The slight figure stiffened. Someone had recognized him! A faint smile curved his lips, but no sound passed. Was not he, Zorro, this moment engaged on a secret mission? Had he not risked daylight to find the best, the keenest of swords?

We turned into Woolworths.

The crowd in the aisle parted. A woman gasped. The child beside her cried, "Look, Ma! It's Zorro!"

Look Ma, I thought, my amazement almost eqaling theirs, Zorro it is. Not the real one, of course. That seeming Jekyll-and-Hyde of courage dwelt in the far-off lands of projector and tube.

This 1958 Zorro was our son Brian. He had lived with us peacefully for five years, growing normally from baby to boy, trike to bike, worshipping such distant heroes as Mickey Mouse and Wild Bill "Hiccup."

Suddenly all that vanished, swept into the pallid haze of infancy as finally as rattles and playpen.

Overnight, with my chance purchase of a hat and mask, Brian became the living Spanish Robin Hood. He no longer walked. He skulked, crouched, leaped. He slid around house corners, vaulted fences. He pounced at us from counter height, preferably when we were carrying a full load of dishes.

He ate with us — masked. Nightly, when he went to bed, 10 minutes of thumps and scrapings warned us not to try his barricaded door. We might discover who Zorro really was.

As Brian's preoccupation with the role grew, so did his demands. He needed a cape. I cut up a good black skirt. He required a mustache. Since he couldn't naturally grow one, he raided my mascara. Daily the supply dwindled. What remained was balled in sticky blobs, resembling a trampled pig-pen after spring rains.

All was not yet perfect. Where was Zorro's sword?

To remedy this intolerable lack we set out for the toy counter. As often happens in the affairs of heroes, the course from first to last was shot with pain.

Erika, our oldest daughter, took one look at the outfit Zorro planned to wear downtown. She screamed.

"MOTHER! You're NOT going to let him go like that!"

"Why not?" I struggled to persuade myself along with her. "He likes it. Do you want to pickle his psyche or something? Just pretend it's Halloween."

"That's years away!" Erika moaned. "I won't be caught dead with him like that!"

A glint lit Brian's eyes. Death. Something Zorro handled neatly. One lunge — and zowie!

"It's him or me!" Erika insisted.

Which was worse, I wondered, her anguish or her grammar? Aloud, I tried to reassure her. "It won't take long to buy the sword."

Erika fixed me with a wordless stare. She knew better. So did I.

I bowed ungraciously to her sensitivities. "So be a coward. Walk behind."

She trailed us, denying any possible connection by 10 feet, a distance causing her to suffer every amused glance and kidding comment. By the time we reached Woolworths, Zorro's sister lagged half a block behind.

At the toy counter I turned to Brian. "Your money?"

Zorro reached for his gold. He handed me 56 cents.

Not bad savings, I reflected, for a five-year-old on a nickel-a-week allowance. Still, Brian, like the well-heeled Don Diego, had always managed funds against a time of need.

He peered darkly through his mask at the swords.

"Here's a nice one," I picked up a six-inch dirk. "Sword, sheat, and plastic cover. All for 29 cents. You'll have money left over."

Zorro looked at it. The plastic kept him from examining it closely. I couldn't see his face, but doubt lay in the tilt of his head.

"Does the sword get longer when you pull it out?"

"No, it's the same length as the sheath."

"I don't want it."

"But it's only 29 cents," I argued.

He looked at me pityingly. "Zorro has a long sword."

"Something like this perhaps?" A passing clerk held up an enormous cardboard with a fencing foil attached. It was magnificent.

The foil stretched all of three feet long. It boasted a crimson grip, yellow hand guard, a wicked, squarish, pliant blade. This last ended in a broad button that widened the sword point for safety and gripped a piece of chalk, which would permit even a kindergarten Zorro to inscribe his exuberant Z on the nearest target in reach.

"I'll take it." Zorro placed his hand on the grip.

"Wait a minute. It's 79 cents," I protested. "You don't have that much."

As casually as Zorro downs an enemy, Brian threw fiscal caution to the floor.

"Forget next week's allowance."

"Brian," I said, dreading his disappointment, "you must understand. If you buy that sword you'll have to give up five weeks' allowance. Not just one. Five."

He hesitated. Under his mustache the smile dimmed. Always before, money in hand had been worth any toy on the shelf. But this was not Brian. I was dealing with Zorro.

"I need this sword." He ripped the weapon from its rubber bands. He whipped it once through the air. Whsst! He flicked a Z on the floor. There it was — backwards — just as he had written it. The smile returned, no longer faint. Now it was sparkling, joyous, totally assured. Zorro the Fox was armed.

I headed for the register, spilling out Brian's savings, digging in my purse for the extra change. When I looked up Zorro had gone. I glanced quickly along the aisle. Was he back admiring the whips?

But Erika stood there, tugging at my sleeve, her cheeks flaming. "Mother! Do something quick! He's out on the sidewalk poking people with that sword!"

I sprinted. No Olympic champ could have done better in a 10 cents store aisle on Saturday afternoon.

Zorro had found his "enemies" and cleared a circle around him. Shoppers smiled — from a distance. One indignant lady, waddling down the street, glared back over her shoulder. There was an interrupted backward Z embellishing her broad behind.

With a firm hold on his cape, I hustled Brian to the car. There followed a loud, stern lecture on the rights and wrongs of handling weapons. Zorro paid no attention. He was intent on thrusting practice. Down went the sword inside his belt. Out it should flick again — only it wouldn't. The chalk button kept catching on his belt. By the time he wiggled it free, Zorro could have been stabbed, unmasked, identified, and laid out with hands at peace on the hilt.

"I need a loop," Zorro announced. "Will you make me a loop?"

I squealed the Chevy around a corner. "What you need," I told him, "is a good swift kick in the cape if you tackle unarmed citizens again." I parked, twisted around to try to confront him. "Listen. We're going in the library next. Are you going to be good, or ... "

"Can I take my sword?"

"Only if you behave!"

Zorro thought it over. "Okay." He leaped from the car, landing with sword at ready. He surveyed the scene.

The old Carnegie public library in Iowa City was ripe for attack. Nothing could be riper. On the outside, a broad balustraded staircase rose to an upper story. Under the staircase, on either side, stood two black grilled iron gates, folded open. To reach the children's section at ground level we had to pass beyond these gates, enter a dim, dank passage, open a heavy glass door, stumble down two unlighted steps, and there we were — in the children's room. If we survived.

Zorro approached the place with the caution it deserved. Perhaps the fat Sergeant Garcia lurked inside?

He sidled to the gate, flattened himself against the stair wall, listened. All was quiet except for one yapping English sparrow. Not quite the game he had in mind. He whipped around the corner into the narrow passage, halted again. No one, nothing was in sight. What could be seen straight out of sunshine into sub-stair-well darkness?

Drawn to his full 44 inches, sword poised, Zorro waited. I heaved open the door. On tiptoe, with shoulders hunched, sword extended, he stole down the steps, then leaped into the hall.

Behind her desk the librarian, Hazel Westgate, let out a squawk.

A smothered titter ran around the room.

Erika vanished behind the nearest book stack.

"Hey, look! Zorro!" someone hissed.

Target of all eyes, Brian straighted up, thrust — after a couple of abortive stabs — his sword under his belt, and stalked in. He ignored the librarian who had recovered her calm, the whispering children. With great dignity, allowing his cape to trail carelessly on the floor, he seated himself at a low table, picked up a book, and began to turn pages slowly.

"Zorro can concentrate. Zorro is good," was the message behind the mask.

Erika and I spent several minutes gathering our weekly armloads of books. Zorro read on. Curious, I glanced over his shoulder to see what rated so much absorption. A tale of his hero, perhaps?

No, it was a book he'd seen before: Polly Cameron's "The Cat Who Thought He Was a Tiger." In it she told the story of a young, inexperienced cat who cuts himself off from his home and family because he believes he's something larger, fiercer, different from his own. Only when he meets a real tiger in his hunt through the world does he learn his true cat nature and return home.

Suddenly, close to my son in the rustle of the warm library, I felt chilled. I stared down at the open book, at Brian's grubby finger tracing the laugh on the caged tiger's face.

In that second I saw his costume for what it was.

"Brian," I longed to cry out, "you're leaving us. This pretending of yours is real. Just like the cat, you've set out trying to find your own self. But a child's search can never be simple. It takes a thousand rough turnings — and the way is not home."

I fought down the impulse to hug him, to tear off that too adult mask and, while there was still time, during this moment of prescience and dread, see for my own reassurance his beloved young face.

Would it have calmed me then if I had known that two decades later this Zorro would grow up to play one of three mimes in off-Broadway's "Mummenschanz," to win praise as the Dying Master in Jim Henson's film "Dark Crystal," that he would enchant thousands of children for five years in roles like Telly Monster and Barkly Dog on "Sesame Street"? And that in 2004, as one of the writers for a children's TV show "Between the Lions," Brian, once alias Zorro, would win a Daytime Emmy?

Maybe. But, especially in raising children, foresight is never around when you need it most.

Frederik Norberg

Supernova

And so it went
My grandmother, a wheatfield of years
The wind howling around her with bells and beeps
And wires calling her name in the antiseptic
Absalom of a gray building, just north of town

She's been in and out the past few days
And I stay close to her
Her Hand breathing into mine
Her eyes closed, then half-open, then closed again
Fighting off the insane gravity of a
Distant world calling her name

"I love you grandma," I say weakly, and then
Turn to the night nurse, who has just checked in
It's all so nothing here, so empty
The smell of unguent, the rattle of the snack trolley,
The wisdom of medicine men scattered on charts
Like ancient runes thrown down

I know the time is coming, when all will be pulled in
And my dark star will leave me, will burst inward
And be pulled into light

I sit bedside, by the lamp
And daydream wheatfields of gray hair.

Dan Campion

Episode

My wife once stood at the kitchen door
Observing a yellow-shafted flicker
Sifting through our lawn, when a
Redtail captured the smaller hunger
And bore it away to the hickory grove.

Today, blue feathers drifting by my window
Convey a fuzzy touch screen shot:
The quota of the Cooper's hawk was met.
A bubble of air distressed in the glass
Glows like the dot of an antique TV set.

The evidence is the mystery:
Sand embracing leaves and bark,
Eddying cilia cast in rock,
Gleaners, stooped by sack or creel,
Sieving tides to scrounge a meal.

Where artery turns vein, stories begin.
Each episode's the molting of a skin,
The curl of a cloud, the dip of a wing
No one sees and when they hear of it
Do not know for precisely what it is.

Precisely what it is is the whole story.
As leafsquall gambles daylight away
Its tent is a temporary cathedral
Pitched where sunsets pink the arch
Of a soaring raptor's prim dihedral.

Patrick McCue

The Artist's Labcoat

Why does scientific progress have to face Mary Shelly? She ruined it with her Doctor Frankenstein and his monster. Progress is not all inner strife and life-consuming consequences though — what about iPods and Gigapets and Tickle Me Elmo? And scientific discovery is not the hopeful, romantic wonder that is splashed throughout the health section of Newsweek.

We think science is a single fixed method for discovery, and technology is implementing it in a way that benefits our society on a grand scale — a scale with salvation on one end and apocalypse on the other. The only thing missing is any middle ground. Science is more separate from reality than ever before, yet we demand that it solve the very real problems of our world. Asking science to make this stretch is impossible within its current framework, but we ask because we want progress even if that means chasing the monster until death.

If we want science to progress in a helpful way we must reconcile its differences with creativity and soften its ties to the profit hungry objectivity that requires perfection. Science will move forward and benefit everyone if it can rest gently among economics and literature and art. And science will progress without the terror of irreversible consequences or the criticism facing seemingly trifle, purely academic achievements when it can be observed through an electron microscope, a novel, and a finance report equally.

Shelly begins with science. Frankenstein uses physical science, the oldest, most Newtonian, reputable, Old Boys' Club, hard science, to create his monster. Science is the beginning because it makes sense, but Shelly quickly departs from this step-by-step rational method in favor of psychological struggles. Imagination-driven, conscience-prodding mental anguish takes hold of her story. Shelly has incorporated science with humanities, but she is rare.

Science has never been the biggest fan of books without charts, graphs, and pounds upon pounds of significant figures all lined up in orderly rows — left to right, top to bottom. Literature hasn't been reaching out to science either. The accepted behavior calls for flowery language or succinct prose scouring human relationships and love for their deeper meanings.

Science is the home of figures, objectivity, and Truth, and literature claims soul-searching questions and romance.

And all of those doctors without borders hippies are romanticizing medicine. They're using old technology to save the world. Good for them, but when it comes down to it we cannot think about stepping back and relying on out-of-date science to save a few lives in Africa when there are improvements to be made here. Good for them for slowing our progression and weighing down our bottom line. Science is a business. Medicine is a business. People think it's okay when technology is allowed that distinction — but not science!

Science is for everyone so they can know the world. I want my kids to look at bugs without having to consider economics. My surgeon shouldn't be wondering how a possible failure due to my dire situation might strike a blow to his future salary when I'm a statistic on his scorecard. Medicine is for the world. Hospitals are supposed to be benevolent and smell like cheap food and antiseptic, but the aroma of Starbucks is filling the air. Parking structures and new specialized wings encase the hometown clinic that once sent doctors out on house calls.

Stop! Science is supposed to be about curiosity, the wonders of the world, and healing people. Helping people.

No —

It's about grants and pharmaceuticals and rich insurance companies and malpractice suits. It's economics; if there isn't a bag of money inside when they open you up, you're being stapled back together — staples are cheaper and faster than stitches. Once you're out, another money bearing consumer is coming in to finance your physician's med school loans.

He has his undergrad at Notre Dame. A Johns Hopkins MD and a father of repute. The cancer center at Harvard's hospital is named after his grandfather, and he was valedictorian in high school, graduated from college Summa Cum Laude. Duke was lucky enough to host him for his residency. He wears Gucci suits and Cole Haan loafers. He is practically a Kennedy, a Carnegie, a Vanderbilt, a Rockefeller. It doesn't matter which name he has as long as he is known — and widely known.

We want doctors of the most venerable pedigree and Ivy League scientists who sleep in white lab coats dreaming of oxidization reactions. If we do not have the best scientists in the world we might not be moving forward when everyone else is. Our scientists should always have science at the top of their minds and doctors and engineers must be single-mindedly applying the new science to technology that will revolutionize the world.

But Einstein was a patent office clerk and Darwin was looking for a free ride vacation. They were well schooled but lived in the world, not the lab. Scientists like this are a dying breed. Now they must move from one white walled lab to another thinking about calculus and salivating over new electron microscopes. Newton was searching for the existence of God through his science, and Einstein saw fairytales as the key to raise America to the top of the scientific world. They knew there was more. They felt it.

They stand in the air conditioned lab poking and prodding their work encased within sealed Plexiglas boxes. Fumbling with sanitized metal instruments grasped in impenetrable rubber gloves is the new way of research. Push the Petri dish into the machine and publish the results as they spew out on endless ribbons of paper, then sit at home this weekend marveling at the lists of numbers and the host of multisyllabic words that jump off the page of the medical journals, all shouting out the cutting edge of science. We have arrived!

But scientists need to feel their work. The status quo calls for separation from the scientist and his or her work. It calls for a disconnect, but this tells us nothing. Scientists need to be connected to their work. Newton imbibed enough lead to kill a small elephant, as the story goes. Lavoisier did the same. Even Darwin tasted his chemicals. After staring at the sun for as long as he could, Newton went blind for weeks before regaining sight. But he did it anyway because he had an insatiable hunger to know what would happen.

"But safety! Where is the safety?" they cry. Of course protocol won't adopt lead milkshakes on the lunch menu at the cafeteria, but walk around in the open air and pick up bugs and feel the mud under your feet. Ask your patient how he's doing — ask for more than a 1 to 10 rating on his pain scale. Ask for more information than choosing the smiley face that best describes his feelings. How are the kids? The job? Embrace your science. Love your patients. And know both intimately.

All imaginary creations and cutting edge technologies are merely reconfigurations of things we already know. And we know because of science. Science shows us how the world works and provides a logical explanation of why it works that way. We want more, though. We want monsters and sea beasts and fairies. Our world should be filled with the Easter Bunny and Santa Claus and leprechauns and castles floating in the clouds. All of these — anything from our imagination — come from what we know. Our imagination never creates anything new, it allows everything we have tasted, felt, smelled, heard, and seen to mix and match and create something we call "new."

This imaginative mixing and matching is a vital element to life and to progress, but it is only possible with science. It is only possible with ecologists' observations and physicists' theories. When we push science past the laboratory we create technology. And that is pushing us forward. If we can allow science not only to allow beauty and poetry but work with it, we will find the answers to the same questions that the humanities and sciences each exclusively call their own.

Don't let the monster frighten scientific progress to a halt. But never progress without considering what monster you will create. Stand up and progress and call science what you will and you will be right. Stand out and point forward and they will line up behind you once progression is definite. Until then, simply stand up and look around a bit.

Kathryn Welsh

Forza Roma

■ ■ ■

Even though we arrived in Rome four days after the city's team had won the National Soccer Championship in June 2001, it seemed as if the victory had just been announced. Crimson and gold, Rome's team colors, were everywhere.

Crimson and gold banners were strung diagonally across the streets. The balconies were draped with crimson and gold flags portraying the legendary she-wolf suckling Romulus and Remus, Rome's twin founders. Revelers were swarming in the streets, cloaked in crimson and gold flags and scarves, riding mopeds and cars while tooting a tune reminiscent of a Ramones leitmotif. The narrow thoroughfares were so frenzied that it took me days to work up the courage to cross any of them without giving my fiancé's forearm a tourniquet-like grip with one hand and sinking the nails of my other hand deeply into his biceps. Instinctively, I sensed I would not be spared if I got in the way of Roman soccer fans and their celebration. It had been 18 years since the Romans had won the Scudetto, Italy's national soccer championship. The victory is awarded to the team that scores the most goals in the season. That year it was Rome 75, Juventus 73, and Lazio 69. They had had 18 long years of never-wavering loyalty to the team while waiting for this, Rome's third national victory. The younger generation had never known this euphoria, the middle-aged were grateful for the chance to bask in the glory a second time, and the older generation stayed at home tending the fire so that everyone else could take part in the festivities. The day after we arrived a waitress at a local trattoria where we had had lunch complained about the late-night mayhem and breaking of glass when the victory was hardly fresh anymore. Before I realized the depth and breadth of the victory celebration (i.e. that it would continue for our entire trip), I snapped a photo of two elementary-aged school boys waving the Roman flag back and forth across their balcony. When they realized what I was doing, they starting posing and implored me, "Keep taking my picture, Signora."

Amidst this national soccer championship glory over arch-rival Lazio, the province in which Rome is situated, we continued our sightseeing and people-watching. Just when we were wondering whether the partying was ever going to cease, we realized that the climax was yet to come. It was to take place that Sunday evening at the Circus Maximus, where in antiquity the chariot races had been held, bets had been laid, and Ovid in the Ars Amatoria had recommended it as " ... a place where nobody will prevent you from sitting next to a girl ..." It is a flat narrow valley that flanks the southern slope of the Palatine Hill. In its prime of chariot racing, the Circus Maximus could hold 150,000-200,000 spectators. Even now when you go by it, you can almost feel the excitement of the ancient races with its helmeted riders racing around the circus for fame and fortune. It seemed ironic that the Romans of these modern times, disenfranchised with an ever-changing government that fails to keep the youth gainfully employed, have channeled all of their patriotism into football and now were about to hold their victory celebration at Caesar's legendary Circus.

The show, scheduled to last more than six hours, was to feature two headline entertainment acts. The first was a concert by a somewhat aged, yet still-revered pop singer, Antonello Venditti. The second act was to be performed by the infamously sexy Roman actress, Sabrina Ferilli. Ms. Ferilli was merely keeping her promise, which she had made in the spring, to the citizens of Rome. If the team brought home the Scudetto, she would entertain them with a striptease. The same city that sent its busy-body old women after me for wearing modestly-cut shorts in the Church of Santa Maria Maggiore was hosting a nationally-televised striptease in front of a live audience of what was to be over a million fans.

All this was to take place in close proximity to where over 1,500 years ago, a monk named Telemachus threw himself into the arena of the Coliseum to break up the fighting gladiators in protest of the barbarous human slaughter. On our flight over, my fiancé had read an Italian news article addressing the controversial upcoming striptease. The Romans and the Church definitely seemed to be divided on this issue. Ms. Ferilli was a loyal "Romana de Roma." Besides, it was her party and she could do as she wanted. (Ms. Ferilli was footing the bill for the entire celebration.) However, the Church obviously did not want such a public display of carnal desires. We could not help but wonder if any one of the thousands of clergy or nuns in the Holy City would claw their way through the audience of over a million people and throw themselves down in front of Sabrina Ferilli to protest this particular brand of barbarism. Needless to say, we waited and watched with much anticipation from the safety of our apartment on the Gianicolo as the historical event unfolded on our television screen.

Shortly after the beginning of the program, it became obvious that the number of spectators was far greater than what the municipal authorities had expected. Before the night was over, they conceded defeat and even sent the bus drivers home early in an attempt to unclog the impassable streets.

Venditti's performance spanned the length of the show but was interspersed with other acts such as Corrado Buzzanti singing a piano solo that went, "… We will make love at the exit of the belt highway and if we conceive a daughter we will call her Roma…," parodying a well-known song by Lucio Dalla. This was met with thunderous applause; I would call it Italian high-risk sex, especially in Rome where traffic is unrelenting even without a national soccer championship.

During this pre-strip show, unexpectedly the president of the Roman soccer team came out onto the runway of the stage. He was a short, slightly round-shouldered, and overweight man of 60-plus years wearing a suit on that sweltering night in late June. He appealed over the microphone for some 10,000 Romanisti who had climbed up onto the Palatine ruins, the rooftop of St. Anastasia, and the archeological museum, to get down. His pleas fell on deaf ears as none of the squatters moved. Venditti then took the mike and began chastising the fans in an irritated tone for being so ill-behaved and for their bravado lack of compliance. Then he engaged the rest of the audience in a chant of "get-down get-down get-down" and even singled out a few of the squatters by dress, "Hey, you in the white T-shirt, don't hide your face…." He went on to blame the transgressors for an incident a few weeks earlier that had almost cost Rome this championship. Apparently some overzealous fans had invaded the field five minutes before the end of the pre-championship game, when it had become obvious Rome would win. In their unbridled celebration they stripped the Roman players of their uniforms leaving some of them in their underwear. The charging of the field was an infraction for which the referees could have called the game a draw, forcing a rematch. But in the end, fearing mob violence, they did not dare. Ultimately, Venditti's tongue-lashing had the desired effect. The fans did get down, including the women in spiked heels who were walking on the roof of The House of Augustus.

After the unexpected intermission, the show continued with some more Venditti pop songs. Then the studs were brought out to the runway; seven members of the championship team and some of their women. Among the seven was the captain and star of these "Italian Stallions," Francesco Totti, number 10. They paraded out to the end of the runway where they stood on display, like the finest pieces Michelangelo could ever carve. Fans wafted crimson and gold scarves and flags up to the team so that they could adorn themselves. The soccer players remained silent but grinning, hands on hips or arms folded across chests while the crowd went absolutely wild. There were more than 10 minutes of uninterrupted applause, whistles, cheers, and shouts. Eventually, the team sauntered back down the runway, and the show continued.

After a few more filler pop songs by Venditti, some of them American covers, the final act began. First the scantily clad performers came out and did a dance routine to Kool and the Gang's "Celebrate." A song, which until then I had associated with the first Clinton inaugural ball. The men were wearing short kilt-like skirts with slits up the sides over visible black jock straps. In addition, they each wore a matching black band around their chests with a crimson and gold coat of arms over their left nipples. The women were wearing headscarves, bikini tops, and long sheer crimson and gold handkerchief skirts. There was even a ribbon routine in which the synchronized dancers twirled crimson and gold strips of cloth in time with the music.

Dramatically the music then switched to Carl Orf's "O Fortuna" and smoke filled the stage. From the smoke emerged four masked male she-wolves, each sporting six bare breasts and carrying Ms. Ferilli on a transparent plastic litter that resembled a piece of lawn furniture. The she-wolves' teats jiggled in unison while they transported a languishing Ms. Ferilli down the runway. The actress was wearing a long white kimono-like robe. Her escorts set her down and she descended from her throne to greet her people. At first her act was all arms waving to the crowd as if to thank them for coming to the "party." Then she disrobed down to her second layer. This layer was long and sleek, a dark green sleeveless dress. In this part of her routine the crowd became more frenetic and Ms. Ferilli gave us even more smiles and twirls. Some of the more innovative fans were holding up a very large white sign that spanned between two handmade goal posts and read in bold letters "SABRINA GOAL." It was as if she, not Totti, were responsible for winning the championship. Next, she untied her green dress-like robe and proceeded to open it to the crowd; they screamed madly. Underneath she was wearing a short, sleeveless, skimpy red dress with thigh-high tan leather boots and spiked heels. She stepped forward out of the robe and she gave us not only smiles and twirls but a few high kicks too.

Then Ms. Ferilli ran back down the runway to be shielded by a human curtain composed of the masked-male she-wolves while she prepared for her final tease. Smoke once again filled the stage and we waited anxiously to see where she would appear next. Suddenly, she burst out of the smoke onto the runway. The crowd went berserk. They were waving banners and scarves fast and furiously as Ms. Ferilli graciously made her way down the runway in her final outfit. She was carrying the Roman flag on a pole and sporting a very wide smile. Ms. Ferilli was in a flesh-colored thong bikini with pasties, rhinestone straps, and the thigh-high tan-leather boots with spiked heels and pointed toes. At the end of the runway she stopped and allowed the crowd to enjoy her body for a few more minutes before she again disappeared. Moments later, she reappeared in an open-weave dark dress that left the bikini visible on the arm of Venditti. He paraded her around on stage, admiring her beauty while chiding her about having made the priests of Rome so nervous.

Dannye Seager Frerichs

A Morning for Growing Older

You stand in the corner of the kitchen,
tall in your T-shirt and shorts.
Somehow those are not the summer things they were last week
but now the crisper, cooler clothes of First Grade.
I take your picture.
And then you turn, hide your summer-stretched back
beneath a backpack full of unwritten pages.
This is a morning for growing older.

Later I sit out on the bench beside the house.
We have managed to catch the last bit of the fleeing summer, your sisters and I!
It tried to disappear around the corner like a silenced ice cream truck,
but we've trapped it up between the fence and house,
and we wet it down with water shooting from the sprinkler.
Summer loves to get wet.
Somewhere inside of me, I am dancing on the lawn with the twins,
damp and hot and cold at the same time.
For us, it is a morning for being four years old
forever.

Suzanne Cody

Why We Choose Who We Choose

■ ■ ■

We had been riding in cars together for eight years, at this particular point in time, this post-Christmas night, on our way home to New York City after spending maybe one too many days with our respective families. At 22, eight years seemed like eternity, like we had been friends riding in various vehicles in various states of sobriety for all of time.

Mickey, a Poughkeepsie society matron by default, has two dark-haired, fair-skinned, almond-eyed children, now. I, on the other hand, am a chaotic and chronically broke single mother of one Mediterranean girl-child. Though thrust into adulthood by our various progeny, we attempt to maintain our shared black sense of humor.

On the phone, to me: "Whose idea was this damn kid-thing, anyway?"

"You had to go and get married and have the first one — and then you went and had another. Don't even start."

Mickey was, is, "Mom" to me, forever my storm port between crises — drug nightmares, psychic meltdowns, suicide attempts, hospital stays, relationship breakups, unwanted pregnancies — she was, is, always on the other end of the phone. On the flip side, I have been consistent, have been "always," in only two things: my chaos, and my love for her. She could give Jesus lessons in patience. She is the first family I chose.

I arrived on her doorstep in New York City after experiencing spectacular relationship failure in Iowa City, complete with unfounded accusations of infidelity, rapidly packed suitcases, teary phone calls from airports — all the delicious drama. I called Mickey. She paid for a plane ticket, I flew to New York, and she settled me in with hot tea and cold beer and lots of cigarettes, waiting patiently for my sanity to reach apartment-leaving, job-finding levels. This had yet to happen, as even crossing the street to get cigarettes from the corner bodega was more than my tender psyche was prepared to handle.

Mickey brought me cigarettes when she came home from work — she worked for, of all people, Michael Forbes, mostly picking up dry-cleaning and reminding him to call his mother. Over dinner I told her stories of people I had seen through the windows on 2nd Avenue: "This woman was so Michael Jackson in drag, she even had the glove and the Jheri-curls. And this little dog that peed on people's feet. How Michael Jackson is that?"

"So ... you're telling me you saw Diana Ross?"

She left money in the mirror frame over her bureau on the off chance I did manage to go out. She left me her number at work in case, God forbid, I should get lost crossing the street to the bodega, or my ex called to "talk" and made me frantic, or the pills in the bathroom cabinet started to look too enticing. I called and called and called. "Hi, honey, how's your day going? Type any thrilling memos?"

"I had to call Bill Gates. You want to go on a date with him? He's Mr. Forbes 500 Eligible Bachelor ..."

"Ergh, Jesus, no thanks. I know all about that blanket thing on airplanes. Oh, can you get me cigarettes? Do you want me to burn you something for dinner?"

"No, no, don't try to cook anything. I'll make something when I get home."

"Oh, come on, that fire was so not my fault."

She cooked me macrobiotic meals. She walked for miles with me all over the icy city listening to my street-corner-preacher-rants about what she referred to as my Howard Stern Show love life. She rented the car so we could drive home to our profoundly rural Maine hometown to see our profoundly dysfunctional families for the holidays.

Two days after arriving and at least ten half-hysterical phone calls later, salvation arrived in my driveway armed with cigarettes, food, and about fifty Grateful Dead bootlegs. "Mick, my family is insane," I said, tumbling into the passenger seat of our delightfully monkey-shit brown sedan.

"Yes," she said.

I reached toward her. "Hey, guess what?"

"What?" She hugged me back, tight.

"We get to go home now, Mama."

"Yes," she said, as I gently tugged the spikes out of her hands and feet.

It was late when we left and rapidly got later. One in the morning flowed into two into three and there was not another car for miles. We drove south, away — drunken, controlling, neglectful parents and angry, abandoned, sad siblings taking their proper places on the far back burners, bubbling quietly to overflow another day.

We listened to tape after tape, sometimes singing, sometimes silent, wrapped up in the warm comfort of knowing home was our destination. "Allman Brothers or David Bowie?"

"David Bowie? Hot Tuna."

"John Prine."

"Talking Heads."

"Dead."

"Okay, which one?"

Brought-from-home kindergarten snacks (carrot sticks dipped in tahini, rice cakes, apples, whole wheat pita bread and almond butter) were balanced by truck-stop sodas and bags of chips and many, many cigarettes.

The moon rolled across the sky like a cue ball out of a Tom Waits song, reflecting blue on the snow blanketing both sides of the highway. I-95 is a good road, a classic highway in the most New England sense — not braggy, loud Route 66, or self-absorbed, too-cool-for-its-own-good Highway 1 up the California coast. I-95 wants to get from one place to another with a minimum of fuss and has contentedly transported New Englanders north and south since Jesus left Chicago, or maybe some time shortly after that. After the naked fields of the Midwest, I was happy to be enclosed by evergreen trees and blasted walls of rock. It was safe, cozy and contained, like returning to the womb.

"Get your feet back in here. You're going to catch pneumonia, or get frostbite, or something." She fumbled with her pack of Marlboros, and I considered my options.

"I'm good, I'm good, I'm fine, I have two pairs of socks on ... just turn the music back up, please? Like right now, maybe?" I handed her my lighter.

She steered with her knee, trying vainly to achieve ignition in the high wind coming through the open window. The speedometer needle hovered somewhere between eighty-five and ninety. "Close the damn window. I'm not turning up the music until that window is closed!"

"Okay, okay, gimme a minute." Struggling with the sticky crank, I managed to shut the wind outside where it belonged. My actually-quite-numb feet, on the other hand, had nowhere to belong. "What the hell is down here?" I reached with both hands under the blood-warm dashboard heater.

"I wouldn't do that if I were you," Mickey mumbled around her finally lit cigarette.

"I'm a big girl, I can handle it."

I worked doggedly at redistribution. The backseat, already overflowing with smeary plastic containers, soda bottles, bits of cellophane and empty cigarette packs received further handfuls of said detritus. Little bits of floating stuff snagged in my wind-tangled hair, in the fluffy wool of my too-big sweater.

Finally settled, I observed with deep fascination as Mickey continued to steer with a left knee that poked like a sharp, pale rock through the sizable hole in her jeans, while working the lighter trying to get her cherry-less smoke restarted. She inhaled, getting a deep lungful. "Okay," she said, breathing out slowly.

Down went the window. Up went the music. The Rent-A-Wreck stereo speakers crackled and thumped under the assault of "Fire on the Mountain." A glowing spark fell to the rough stripy brown fabric of the bucket seat. It was interesting to watch it burn.

Tilting back, I put my freshly warm and now somewhat aromatic wool-socked feet up on the dash, lit a pick-me-up cigarette. No sleeping for me while she drove. A chronic non-driver, my sole trip-contribution was keeping Mickey awake — well, that, and redistributing detritus and working the tape deck and providing the running comedic commentary when she started to drift too far away into that place she would drift, sometimes. Singing: "Dysfunction Junction, what's your malfunction?" but saying, always, really: "Where did you go? You have to come back, come back, now, because I need you, here." She would laugh, which was always, really, "I'm here, I'm back, I hear you."

I watched her drive, and smoke, watched the wind tug and pull at her long black hair. In the dashboard lights, her lips looked slightly blue. Bone thin, she hated to be cold, but as I couldn't stay awake without the bitter wind watering my eyes we compromised by keeping the heat on full blast, and she wore at least three sweaters over her lanky frame.

Her mouth moved along with a particularly good version of "China Cat Sunflower." Her long, slim hands were like birds, coming to light at her lips, the steering wheel, the ashtray, her lips again in a way I had always envied, being short-fingered and ham-handed myself. She checked the clock on the dash, and, as if we were late for the party, stepped on the gas a little more. The speedometer climbed above ninety. It was like flying. I was being born at light speed.

"This is good," I said.

"What?" Jerry's wail slid down to a whisper.

"I said, 'This is good.'"

"Yes," she said, and turned the music back up.

The moon continued its cue ball path across the sky.

Nick Smith

Mr. Drone

Mr Drone can hold a bee in
either hand and not be stung.
His wife is short
with worts and hives.
Still he calls her
his queen,
his honey bunch,
his honey bee
his honey moon
which only goes to prove
beauty truly is in the eye
of the bee holder.

Krissy Dallmann

Thick Skin

The evening light was starting to go as Em helped her father with the chores. It was autumn, early November. Em filled the last bucket of water for the night and followed her father to the barn. The water sloshed up the sides when she moved, and she tried to match her father's pace.

The barn was on a hill to the west of the farmhouse, 100 feet away from the pump. Em watched her feet and counted her steps, one, two, one, two. In the light of the sunset she looked up, squinting in the glow of orange that hit her face, the buildings, the trees. The shadow of her father grew larger. It reached long and thin until it touched the tops of her shoes. She stopped and put the buckets down, water coming up over the lip and landing on the ground. Em sunk her hands deep in her pockets and pulled out her gloves. She put them on and picked up the buckets again, splashing water on her shoes as she hurried to catch up.

At the top of the hill the barn blocked the remaining sunlight from hitting the cattle lot, and only dark forms were visible. Em knew her father was there, but she couldn't make out his shape. Low bellows rolled along the air like hungry ghosts. Em stood beside the fence where the long feed bunk reached out in front of her. She watched cattle push against themselves for position, their warm bodies packed tight for food. Vapor rose from their collective breath, held by the last rays of light. Her father's buckets were sitting by the fence, solid and cold. Em sat hers next to his and watched her own breath rise from her nostrils.

In the dark of the lot she heard her father's voice, slapping tough hides to make room for himself. He pulled bales of hay from the hayloft, popped off the twine and spread it evenly for the beasts. Soon the outline of her father was visible. He walked across the lot and back to the fence where Em was standing, reached over the top board to grab the buckets that Em lifted up to him. He disappeared again into the darkness. Em moved from one foot to the next as she waited, rubbing her gloves against her sleeves, watching her breath. She looked back to the dark lot and saw a shadow weaving back and forth on uneven ground. Her father took the last two buckets, disappeared once more, and then came back to the fence.

"Tomorrow I'll look into buying a water tank for the lot so we don't have to carry this water anymore." He climbed back over the fence, getting pushed around by the cattle at the feed bunk just on the other side. Em picked up two of the empty buckets and followed her father away from the barn.

"Dad, how come you don't wear any gloves when you do chores?" From the light that was left they were both barely visible, almost lost in the twilight.

"Guess I don't need them, Em."

"But how come I have to wear gloves? How come my hands get cold and yours don't?" The sound of their steps echoed off the buildings, and they seemed bigger than they were.

"Well, I guess my skin is just thicker than yours. That's what happens when you're out here, year after year. Thickens your skin right up. Tough." He slapped the back of his hand a couple of times, and smiled even though Em couldn't see him. She looked over her shoulder at the last strip of light in the sky, blue leading into blue, then darkness to the stars. A sliver of moon accented the night sky, hanging not too far above Em's head.

"Dad, will my hands be tough like yours someday?" Em and her father reached the sidewalk that led to the house, lit by the artificial porch light that stung her eyes.

"Well, Em, that all depends. All depends on how you use them."

Jonathan Starke

I Dun, Uhmannumb

■ ■ ■

2,000 miles. It's how far away I was from home when I first heard the Russian girl talking in the apartment below me. Each night while waiting for sleep, there would be the faintest sound of her Russian voice coming up along the walls and sliding underneath the carpet like it was trapped. Moving so far with just a car and a few hundred dollars doesn't allow a person much to go on. There was no bed. I slept on the floor where the little black bugs crept and scurried out in front of my eyes, my cheek pressed against the carpet listening for her. The eye furthest from the ground could see the clearest, and from so close, the bugs could have been dogs or cats, so close as I've seen dogs or cats before.

Some say life is the same everywhere you go, and I believe that's probably true. Back home there were friends and crutches — good things — and then there were also faces I would see that invoked a false smile when passing on the street, and then once beyond the back of the person my face would go ugly as I put a hand arranged in the shape of a gun against my own temple, hammering the thumb-trigger down a few feet after they passed. Soon, the imaginary brains would splatter to the left of me (as I would shoot right handed) and land on an old lady with tan stockings who wouldn't know what to make of the death face I was putting on, my tongue dangling like a fish on a hook. I just didn't care for that person passing, that person I had seen one too many times. And that's what life was back home; certainties. I was certain that life really was the same wherever a person went, but I was here without those certainties, and my hope that life was not really the same everywhere, that things could be different somewhere else, that was foolish, but a foolishness I wished to maintain.

I watched them scurry behind the baseboards, their black bodies like bee-bees rolling on little hairs. You feel bad for swatting at them with your hand, your head smashed up against the carpet pretending to sleep, but knowing you're just waiting to hear that voice from down below. They would forgive you if they understood; everyone would if they knew where you were in life.

Hunting for jobs wasn't as easy as it was back home either. I can't just go to a friend who works at a CD exchange store and tell him I love CDs and have always wanted to work for a used CD store, and re-case and label and shelve, and have him let his manager know who lets the boss know who sets you up with a part-time going on full-time position. It's not so easy here. My last job was at a book depository so I figured I'd use that as some sort of in, as if that in were a skin and bone friend. "Yeah," I told her, "I used to work at the book depository back home. Almost two years I worked there." Your thought is that your friend, your in, is going to carry you through to the next level just like before. But a week later and I still haven't heard back from the lady manager of the used bookstore. Kristy is what she said her name was. That lady manager Kristy still hasn't gotten back in touch with me.

This morning I woke and stepped into something. It was very early morning, so early it was still dark and the only light was the soft orange behind the curtains from street lamps and alley posts. On the bottom of my foot, stuck to it like a leech, was a sun-flower seed. It was clearly left by the previous tenants (though sometimes, in that world of dream and hope, I sometimes wish it was the little black bugs coming out from the baseboards to offer me a tasty pact, some kind of insect treaty that indirectly stated they would stop crawling on me at night if I'd stop swinging at them with an open palm and open eyes and a cheek pressed against the furry ground they crawl on) but I don't eat those things anymore, not since I was back home playing little league baseball games. Our biggest goal then was to see who could spit the seeds through a certain slanted square in the fencing of the dugout; of course the spitter had to remain in their seat while spitting. We all used the motions of our body to thrust forward like a wave and let the seeds fly. We hardly ever made it through the right hole, but we always said we did. My biggest goal now was to get the seed off my foot and drop it in the nearest garbage can, which I did, which wasn't really a garbage can, but a plastic sack I nabbed from the local grocery store. A person can't afford to spend money on trash cans when they drive so far on a few hundred dollars and an old car. Investments have to be wise and the carpet is clean for now.

I haven't heard the Russian in three days. Night by night, for these two weeks, she's played to me like a tape full of rain and dust and wind; songs for the ears to sleep. Now, in such a mad rush to hear her, I walk past my room and peek in, think I've heard a noise and dive at the floor. No longer do I collapse slowly and softly, allowing my biceps and chest to catch the weight of my body, but I fall down right onto my grandmother's quilt and a few sheets I took from the thrift store (maybe not right onto them, maybe a little off to the side so I can feel the harshness of the rug burn against my body in relation to the softness of a spread blanket).

I walked around the town again today. There are many men with sunglasses and mud spattered bodies who put out their hands and ask for change. I never say "yes" to their begging, but I also am not able to form the correct words to say no. Something is always muttered, ushered out from my lips, but never anything that really makes any sense, just sounds more like a rusty foreign language. It's almost as if I'm muttering just as they are, "Hey, man, could you spare me 50 cents?" and it comes out like a child chewing on a Rubik's Cube. A person scoots off the street a little, maybe into the bike lane if your town has the kind of people my town has. And I get locked right in his dirty eyes when he calls me "man" because it's hard to turn away from someone who's calling out the unique bond you share with each other. I mumble back right after I scoot and set my eyes to something in front, nothing in particular, whatever I can quickly blur for the moment. "I dun, uhman-numb."

Last night the Russian girl was back again. It was one or two, and I was eating cereal from a plastic bag when I heard the apartment door close downstairs. I rolled up the bag and threw it on top of the refrigerator and dove headfirst near the quilt where my bed would be if I had the money. I dove or fell like a seal would into water, like a person might if they were really drunk and didn't care how the floor felt when a body crashed onto it. There was a voice talking with her, a low voice, the voice of a man like my father. I could have envisioned him with slick black hair if the tone and sound wasn't so familiar. In my head he was tall and thin and angular, a contemporary tower, the kind of man who wore his underwear on his head on the way to a morning shower. Now they were arguing or talking quickly, it was too late to know now. I just wanted him to leave so I could hear her voice again singing to the radio or talking to her mother who would be stirring a pot of vegetable beef in her left arm while holding the phone between her ear and crooked shoulder repeating "dah" into the phone all the way from the crooked streets and brown benches of Makhachkala. Nobody could understand now what my father was saying to her. "From Makhachkala with love," says her mother.

The morning usually brings some sort of peace to life. The garbage truck beeps like an electrically charged dawn bird as it makes its descent into the alley and scoops up what remains of who we are, or what we were. I'm usually too sick to eat. I move along the same square of downtown, never stopping long enough to sit or rest, but occasionally, I've found myself making sudden stops just to see another person, to understand that though I think it, though I feel it, I am not utterly alone in this world. There are so many people, so many doors possible for opening that each day is like a set-up, like some sort of opportunity to either be grabbed or lost. I have found that I lose more often than not. Here.

Tonight I was going up the stairwell and I saw the Russian girl. It may not have been her, but she looked as I would think the Russian girl would look. She had black hair and pale skin and was walking barefoot, so bare that anyone could see the tattoo running along the top of her foot and around her ankle. I said to her that it must have hurt, and she looked up at me as if to cry or eulogize my life. "I am not my father," I told her, but she looked at me the same either way. 2,000 miles.

I walked to the bookstore on a rainy day. It had been long past two weeks, and I was told nothing, heard nothing, saw not a thing but myself without a job or a friend. At the desk was a skinny kid with a gray plaid shirt, his hair was black and slick like the Russian man should have been. Except he had a goatee. I asked him for the manager lady named Kristy, and he said she didn't work there. I said, "Anymore?" and he said, "Ever."

I started to think of ways to kill myself. Throwing up is one of the worst feelings a person can have, especially if it's due to an overdose of pills. They save too many people who puke off those things. Guns are too messy, which is cliché, but so true. I wiggled my hands lower on my thighs as I felt the right half of my body on the softness of blanket and the left half on the harshness of carpet. I wobbled like penguins do out of water. No slitting of the wrists, too gory. I couldn't dive off a building because assuredly a freefall wouldn't kill me like it should and I'd somehow be left in a hospital with tubes and monitors and no spine to walk with. But at least I'd finally have a bed.

The Russian girl has been alone. She still sings before entering the shower, and she cleans up late. Sometimes I think it's for my father to come over, but he — the voice — has not been there for so long. I still cannot understand what she says, but I long to go down and see her, to meet her if that wasn't her in the stairwell with the inked foot and the wounded face. I miss the strands of her hair and the way she didn't seem as if she cared for apples. I'm not sure why the body stops demanding food when so little is done during the day. Trying to think, but I'm not sure what I've put down. It would be best to eat something not so close to what humans are, something made from grain sounds about right.

I rented a car storage unit today. It's not open air, but garage, just like we had back at our old place, back at my father's. It was completely necessary to have a garage that was closed and dark where nobody could see in and do anything to the car. It's the only mode of transportation I really have left, long transportation, a way to finally get away from here, the investment that needs protection. It's sealed in there. A person could do whatever they wanted with their car, with the air in that room, that sealed up room.

I am shaking now. I was standing in the shower, under the cold water to shock my brain and body back into life. Something awful has happened. The Russian girl was downstairs, I heard her, and the man came in. He was yelling awful at her in some sort of Russian dialect that was more Russian than anything I'd heard before. When you fear for life, you act in the way that nature prefers, for me it was to act to save (if possible). I grabbed the big kitchen knife, the one I used to cut lamb legs and chicken before I stopped eating so close to humans. Down the stairs I went like a superman of black, wielding the shiny knife that would save her. The Russian man had left the door open and I ran through the entranceway and they were there, tumbling along the ground and she was making hysterical noises. I couldn't feel anymore if it was laughter or pain, though it looked so much like the former. I still got him by the hair and pulled him back against the wall with the knife to his throat and was ready to slit it like the leg of a lamb. But just in that moment, in the moment of choice of life and death and the strings we are allowed to pull as acts of God and fate ourselves, I saw that the Russian girl had red hair and was now crying. She was speaking through her mouth in pure, good, English, but all I could hear was a mix, a jumble of words, something like broken human speech.

Kate Miller

Warmth

I knew it was
Where I belonged.
She was gentle,
And sang softly
As she rocked
In a chair,
By the fire,
At our old
Farm house.
I think I remember
Sitting on her lap.

Patricia Davis

Messages Written, Never Mailed

■ ■ ■

I have one sibling, a brother (Zack) just one year older than I. He's married to a woman named Mimi. They live in New York City part of the year. They have been married a long time but had no children. It just wasn't convenient for their lifestyle. So be it. For the past five years they have stopped to visit us in Florida where we spend the winter and stayed and stayed. Our two youngest sons (we have four) now live in the Big Apple and Zack and Mimi invited them to dinner last Sunday.

This week we received an e-mail from Mimi. She sent three paragraphs of prose. The first paragraph mentioned how good the boys look and what a nice evening they shared.

The second paragraph told us that we could give each son $11,000 this year and we would not have to pay taxes on this gift. We should help enhance our children's lives at every opportunity. My quick math made this $44,000. $44,000 dollars! Is this woman crazy?

The third paragraph mentioned that they had not made any winter plans as yet but would keep us posted.

$44,000 dollars. My God! My demented rage finally gave way to dithering giggles. I wrote a glissando of replies, but never mailed them. Tom (my husband) is calling this my notebook of vitriol.

Reply one: How presumptuous, even for you, to put your pushy fingernails into our private finances. We do not have that kind of money and even if we did, we would use our own discretion (with professional help) on how to spend it. If you feel the boys could use a lump sum the same tax advantage could be used on your money. Go ahead, kick in a bundle to each of them. They could use a hidden blessing and you'll feel great. They probably would even say thanks. Sorry your winter plans are not firm. Maybe this would be a good year to revisit Oregon. Remember how you went there to hide from the millennium staying in that Buddhist Monastery on a 30-day silent retreat? This year you could extend the time to 90 days. Think of all the words you'd save. Keep in touch. Love, Pat

Reply two: How insensitive and tacky for you to try to drive a financial wedge between us and our children. Your life must be so empty and lonely for you to do such a sad thing. An apology will be accepted. Keep in touch. Love, Pat

Reply three: How incredibly kind of you to volunteer to become our financial advisor. Your schedule is so crammed with other volunteer and good deeds I'm not sure when you'd find the time to become our long distance accountant. Should we just send our bank books directly to you and you could put us on a allowance? Then you would be in total control of something, somewhere. What a good feeling that would be. Keep in touch. Love, Pat

Reply four: Thanks so much for providing us with the laugh of the week. Your uninformed and self-inflated notion of our material wealth is something we could strive for in our future endeavors. In the meantime please don't try to wedge a non-existent money stash between us and our children. I think you need a new hobby or cause. Are the homeless all taken care of? Try domestic violence. They need help. Keep in touch. Love, Pat

Reply five: Wow! So good to hear from you. I was wondering what to do with that $50K I had stashed in the Cayman Islands. The Feds are beginning to sniff around. This is perfect. I siphoned this money off the "Feral Cat Shelter" while doing an audit. It was a breeze. The cats are in good hands. I got my contact (Miguel) to smuggle them aboard that garbage barge that's been circling the globe for 16 years. They've never had it so good. Miguel says they are getting plump and their coats look like they've been coated with Crisco. Thanks again. Keep in touch. Love, Pat

Jean Murphy Rude
Not Yet

I'm not ready for Fall
Its sun bowling across
the neighborhoods at five-o-clock.
Sweaters and late squash.
The hair blooming on my horse
Pools emptying like broken
balloons all over the city.
I hadn't finished yet
with Summer. I forgot to
rest at the bottom of
the pool, I forgot to
lie out on the grass. I just
drove, and worked, and
fretted, the seasons twisting
away like stars.

JD Mendenhall

Exercise vs. Working Out: A Tongue-in-cheek Primer

■ ■ ■

Have you ever watched a commercial for a workout facility and been mystified why people would willingly perform such unnatural gyrations and contortions? Have you ever seen a new exercise gizmo and thought it looked more like one those ill-fated flying contraptions in an old newsreel clip? Or have you heard your daughter mention her Pilates class and you've been perplexed by her sudden interest in great philosophers? If you answered "yes" to any of these questions, I can help.

There was a time when people generally got enough exercise from their daily routines, whether it was milking cows, chopping wood, or running from saber-toothed tigers. But those days are long gone, and the most exercise many of us get today is walking from our car to the fast food restaurant or wandering around the house shouting, "Has anybody seen the remote?" So most of us need to make a special effort to exercise.

But exercising on your own can be tough. Many people would be interested in joining some form of organized exercise at a workout facility, but they're scared. Scared of being the heaviest or most out-of-shape person there. Scared they won't be able to do the exercises or operate the equipment. Scared that the spandex pants they squeeze into will snap during a squat and put someone's eye out.

Well, I can't really help if you're the largest person in town or if you somehow manage to wrangle your hind quarters into kids bicycle shorts, but I can offer you some helpful explanations of the current exercise lingo, trends, and equipment:

Spinning — The name simply refers to the spinning of a bicycle wheel and used to be called "riding an exercise bike," which replaced "riding a bike." It doesn't matter if the next transformation of bike riding is called "Schwinning," if somebody doesn't invent a bike seat that's at least as wide as most backsides and as comfortable as a La-Z-Boy, its still going to be mainly a spectator sport.

Pilates — Named for its inventor Joseph Pilates (pronounced puh-la'-tees), these core (see Core) exercises are a lot like pushups and sit-ups with a little yoga (see Yoga) thrown in. I think Pilates sounds more like an appetizer at a fancy restaurant, as in, "Yes, I'll have the pan-seared hatchling with the mashed mangoes, and let's start with an order of the jalapeño pilates."

Personal trainer — This is the person responsible for assessing your exercise needs, developing your specific exercise program, and coaching you through your exercise routine. This is not to be confused, however, with the person who actually has to perform the exercises, which would be you. While your personal trainer will likely become someone you will despise, loathe, and fear, always keep in mind the exorbitant fee you're paying him or her to torture you.

Cardio — Formerly known as "aerobic exercise" until aerobics became tagged as "prancing around in spandex and a headband." As you might suspect, cardio does indeed refer to equipment (such as treadmills) and exercises (such as jumping jacks) designed to exercise your heart. You might not suspect, however, that cardio also refers to which hospital department you'll spend the night in if you perform the entire cardio workout designed by your personal trainer.

Stair climbers — Formerly known as "taking the stairs," these aptly named machines actually mimic climbing stairs. The stair climber machine industry has a very strong lobbying effort in Washington, D.C., which is why in new buildings, the stairs are usually harder to find than Richard Simmons's masculinity.

Ellipticals — Named for the geometric shape they trace with your feet, these machines combine the motions of stair climbing and bike riding. It feels a lot like trying to walk up a downward-moving escalator. Which reminds me of the mall. Which reminds me of the aromatic cinnamon roll place. Oops, forget I even mentioned that, and get back on your machine.

Crunches — This is just the newfangled name for sit-ups, but more suitably describes the sounds your vertebrae make as you lie on your back and try to lift 40 years worth of pizza and ice cream off the floor.

Yoga — A form of low-key exercise characterized by twisting the body into unnatural poses. Said to have been practiced as far back as the Stone Age, yoga experienced a resurgence in the Stoned Age of the 1960s. Also said to be one possible road to inner peace, as are meditation, chanting, and The Cheesecake Factory.

Core — Describes the groups of muscles in your abdomen, lower back, and hips.

Exercising and strengthening your core apparently provides a solid foundation for more advanced exercises such as "picking the kids' socks up off the floor" and "clipping your toenails." You've also heard it referenced in "rotten to the core" (which may require an anti-diarrheal.)

Giant exercise balls — The most enjoyable addition to the "exercise ball" category since the medicine ball, giant exercise balls are used to sit on or lie on while performing exercises, just in case you don't have enough balance issues already. The giant rubber balls also prove quite advantageous if you ever find yourself playing dodge ball with a room full of 4-year olds.

Individual flat-screen monitors — Designed to take your mind off the fact that you are exercising, these are simply little televisions attached to your cardio machine so you can watch Oprah, CNN, or commercials for workout facilities. I'm all for taking my mind off my impending collapse, but isn't sitting in front of the TV one of the main reasons most of us need more exercise?

Cool down — Ideally, at the end of the workout, you're supposed to calm yourself, gently stretch, and cool down. I, however, collapse onto my back, clutch my chest, and gasp for air. Choose the cool down method that works best for you.

You now have all the information you need to walk into that new workout facility and declare, "I've got a coupon for 15 percent off, and that better refer to my weight as well." So whether you end up all buff, or just in the buff under your hospital gown, you'll have me to thank.

Matthew Black
Nothing But A Smile For Mrs. Marken

late August heat redefines all we momentarily understood
so we sit bored on the burning
concrete steps outside the city pool
— closed for the summer a week ago —
discrete scent of Lilies in the air

[for an instant I think it might just be your fragrance]

but tracing it back through the breeze I realize it's
coming from Mrs. Marken's flower garden

I am not let down
still, strangely enough, a damper creeps over

"So those Romans sure are cursing a lot these days"
I say hopefully to your approval
but you misunderstood "cursing" as the opposite of blessing
instead of my simple thoughts of vulgar speechless

but I am not let down
because I suppose that they may be
doing that as well

take no time to clarify
just retrace sidewalk cracks
back through time to some day in early April
when we were surely asking:

if we could fly around this town what would we see?
if we could walk through walls where would we be?
if we could read minds would we think
"what strange powers we wish ourselves to possess?"
The ability to look deeper
the sun in a flower

Rick Zollo

Wallace for President

When the oral historian and book writer Studs Terkel turned 95 in May 2007, he lamented American ignorance of its history and its great historical figures. He singled out Iowa's Henry Wallace, in particular. As he told Amy Goodman of Pacifica Radio's Democracy Now, "they [the American public] know Mike Wallace. They know the name, perhaps, George Wallace, but not Henry Wallace."* Studs then linked the former vice president and candidate for the 1948 presidency with such Americans as Abraham Lincoln, Franklin D. Roosevelt, and Martin Luther King. Though the 1999 biography, American Dreamer, by former Senator John Culver and reporter John Hyde, did much to bring Wallace's name back to public attention, the sad truth is most Iowans — as well as Americans — know very little about this man. Yet Henry Wallace was an Iowan who could have been president, should have been president had millions of Americans had their way. He was denied a second term as Franklin Roosevelt's vice president by a cabal of Southern conservative Democrats (later to be known as "Dixiecrats"). Roosevelt died two months into his fourth term; instead of Wallace as president, the nation had the inexperienced Harry Truman at the helm. Truly, history could have been changed had Wallace become president. Instead, he is a trivia question that many Iowans cannot answer. Just who was Henry Wallace?

Before answering that question, let us acknowledge Iowa's only native-born president. Most Iowans know that person to be Herbert Hoover. An excellent presidential library honoring Hoover can be found in Hoover's birthplace, West Branch. Hoover, though, left Iowa in his 11th year, never to live in the state again. Henry Wallace lived for 45 years in Iowa, and was an important journalist, farmer, and farm scientist during his Iowa years.

Wallace was born in 1888 in rural Adair County, an area west of Des Moines. He was a third generation Iowan born to a family that not only farmed but also worked in farm advocacy. His grandfather, also Henry Wallace, was a preacher, farmer, and farm journalist. His father, Harry Wallace, farmed and was founder of Wallaces' Farmer, which he created so Henry Sr. could have a vehicle for his progressive Republican views. Both men were friends and followers of Teddy Roosevelt, the progressive Republican president. Harry Wallace later became Secretary of Agriculture under Warren G. Harding. His enemy at Commerce was the redoubtable Herbert Hoover.

Henry A. Wallace was raised on farms, destined for farm journalism and advocacy, and developed a love for science, which he applied in radical ways. Wallace attended Iowa State College, leaving in 1910 to work on the family magazine. When his father died while serving in Washington, the son was convinced Harry Wallace was killed because of internecine battles with the Secretary of Commerce. Hoover and the Wallace family were to remain bitter enemies to the end.

Harding also died in office and was replaced by Calvin Coolidge. When Coolidge retired, Hoover ran on the Republican ticket during the 1928 election. Henry A. was so much against Hoover's candidacy that he did the extraordinary: he campaigned for the Democrat, Al Smith. The reason was simple yet complex. Farmers had been in an economic depression since the early 1920s. The Wallace family, through their magazine, called for government regulation of supply and demand, and wanted price controls as well as production limits. The Wallaces lamented soil erosion, and believed farmers overproduced in a competitive environment. Hoover, a laissez faire conservative, did not believe in government controls or regulation.

When the stock market crash and subsequent depression brought the nation's financial and manufacturing sectors to the same level as agriculture, Hoover's days were numbered. Franklin Roosevelt summoned Henry A. Wallace to his home in Hyde Park. Wallace listened to Roosevelt's ideas, and shared with him what he thought should be done to assist farmers. Then he campaigned for Roosevelt and was rewarded by being named Roosevelt's Secretary of Agriculture. Wallace was still a registered Republican.

For Roosevelt's first two terms, Wallace led agriculture to a renaissance, and was considered the heart and soul of F.D.R.'s New Deal. Roosevelt's administration brought a government activism to the aid of America's economy. The state of U.S. agriculture as we have known it for the past 75 years was formed under Henry A. Wallace's leadership. His role in Roosevelt's presidency made him one of the leaders of liberal America. When Roosevelt chose him as his vice president in 1940, southern Dixiecrats rebelled. Roosevelt told them it was Wallace or no one; F.D.R. would rather retire than continue without him.

Thus Wallace served as V.P. during America's entry into World War II. He was an ardent internationalist. His family had always believed in free trade, and they had predicted a world recession after the country applied tariffs following World War

I. Wallace's time at Agriculture broadened his knowledge of working class America and of the sufferings of the country's underclass. Wallace had been raised Presbyterian, but had become something of a mystic later in life, a follower of Emerson and the transcendentalists. (Today, his religious beliefs would be described as "New Age-y.") As a result, Wallace developed his one-world beliefs, turning away from nationalism and parochial religion, and toward a more utopian philosophy. The one thing Henry Wallace was not was a politician.

And perhaps that was his downfall. In 1944, the very conservative Democrats who had opposed his selection as vice president arrayed themselves against his re-election. F.D.R. was running for an unprecedented fourth term. He was very sick with heart disease, as well as myriad other health problems resulting from the onset of polio that had struck Roosevelt during the prime of his life. Whoever was chosen V.P. would surely become the country's next president.

At first, Wallace's enemies had too many candidates to replace him. Byrne of South Carolina was the favorite, but as an arch segregationist, he would not appeal to Northerners or African Americans. Wallace was the favorite among registered Democrats, but his replacement would be chosen by the proverbial "smoke-filled room." The party hacks that filled that room chose Harry Truman as Wallace's successor.

So Harry Truman followed Roosevelt, and Wallace moved to Commerce, Herbert Hoover's old stomping ground. After Truman ended World War II by dropping atomic bombs on the Japanese cities of Hiroshima and Nagasaki, he led postwar America into a Cold War and arms race with Russia. And there is where history might have been different had Wallace been president.

Wallace had supported America's entry into World War II. He was an anti-fascist who knew the German-Italian-Japanese axis had to be defeated. He had spoken out against Russian communism, but knew the Allied powers needed Soviet support to defeat the Axis. Wallace also had been party to the development of the atomic bomb. Would he have used it on Japanese cities once Germany had surrendered?

Many of Wallace's supporters didn't seem to think so. They believed he would have followed Albert Einstein's hope that the bomb should have been dropped in the ocean as a warning. As Studs Terkel told Amy Goodman, "Einstein felt at the very end, he never dreamed bombs would be dropped on human beings in Hiroshima. He thought they would be dropped on the wide Pacific."*

Einstein, father of the Atomic Age, and Robert Oppenheimer, the scientist who led the research team at Los Alamos that created the bomb, came to regret their participation in the making of the atomic bomb. Keep in mind that 70,000 to 80,000 people, mostly civilians, died in the initial Hiroshima explosion.

Had Wallace been president, he would have tried to resist the call to use the bomb on Hiroshima. He might have been persuaded, however, that the bomb would quickly end the war and maybe save more casualties in the long run. That is a debatable point. I don't believe Wallace would have ordered the dropping of the second bomb on the city of Nagasaki (which killed an estimated 40,000 people in the initial blast). Many historians believe the second bomb was dropped to send a message to our ally, the Soviet Union.

After the war, from his position as Secretary of Commerce, Wallace recommended that our atomic research be shared with the rest of the world. He cautioned against sharing our manufacturing know-how, but he believed the rest of the world's powers, including the Soviets, would want this bomb and would initiate an arms race rather than allow only the U.S. to have this capability. Truman's Secretary of State, Henry Stimson, agreed with Wallace, but was soon replaced by Wallace's political adversary, James Byrne of South Carolina.

Wallace felt that atomic energy should be put to peaceful uses, and not used as a military tool. He advocated cooperation with the Soviets, rather than confrontation. Wallace, who would later vote for Dwight Eisenhower for president, supported General Eisenhower's moderate views about the potential arms race. Had Wallace been president, he would have resisted calls to re-arm the nation and set up military bases that encircled the Soviets. It was Wallace's belief that America provoked the Cold War. Wallace would have preferred more cooperation with the United Nations, and more effort at developing a peacetime economy that stressed full employment and growth in the farm and manufacturing sectors.

Here, an irony comes into play: Henry Wallace was considered a communist sympathizer and a closet socialist during his '48 run for the presidency. No question Wallace was a Social Democrat who believed in an activist government that helped small farmers and factory workers. He was a free trader who fought against special interests. But he could hardly be called anti-capitalist, for during his Iowa years, he led the agriculture revolution in hybrid corn, and set up a for-profit business, Pioneer Hi-Bred, to sell his brand of hybrid corn seed. (When Wallace's heirs sold their share of the business in 1990s, their company's worth was in the billions.) Wallace believed in small business as strongly as he believed in workers' rights. His call in one of his books for the Century of the Common Man was a belief that the world could find peace and prosperity only so long as everyone had a share.

As the Cold War took shape during the latter part of 1946, Wallace's days in the Truman administration were numbered. Byrne was a conservative, and as Truman's new Secretary of State, he embraced the Cold War. Wallace was asked to resign. (He was the last of Roosevelt's New Dealers to leave the Truman administration.) As right wing Democrats and Republicans looked for communists in every boardroom, bedroom, and individual closet, the McCarthy Age took hold. Wallace was considered a naïve idealist who clung to impractical liberal beliefs. And to support those beliefs, Wallace opposed Truman in the historic 1948 election.

This third (or fourth) party run doomed him to political irrelevancy. It can be likened to Ralph Nader's campaigns of 2000 and 2004. The Dixiecrats put up their own candidate, the segregationist Strom Thurmond. New York Governor Thomas Dewey, a friend of Wall Street, ran as a Republican centrist, and seemed unbeatable. Truman was beleaguered. Not only had anticommunism become an infectious disease, Truman had gotten the U.S. into a war on the Korean peninsula to fight communists.

Truman ran a valiant campaign. Wallace was abandoned by anticommunist liberals, such as former allies Claude Pepper, senator from Florida, and Hubert Humphrey, mayor of Minneapolis and soon-to-be senator from Minnesota. Wallace truly did become a tool of America's tiny far leftwing. Studs Terkel, later blacklisted from television by the McCarthyites, was among that small faction.

Wallace's chance at the presidency had come in '44, and he had been denied. He was a stubborn idealist who some felt was a bitter man. His '48 campaign had a Nader-like desperation. The man who should have been president would have perhaps been better off taking the Al Gore path and counseling from the sidelines. Truman won, McCarthy and his ilk continued their demagoguery, and the Korean War became the template for the Vietnam and Iraq quagmires. Centrist Dwight Eisenhower ran in 1952 as a former general who could end the Korean conflict. His presidency also put a damper on the anticommunist disease. (Eisenhower ended his presidency with a speech warning the nation of its military-industrial complex. His belated recognition had a Henry Wallace-like echo that the nation refused to heed.)

Wallace by that time had retired from politics to a farm in Westchester County, N.Y. He did not return to his native Iowa, but he continued to farm and experiment with plants. His work in hybrid strawberry production and crossbreeding of chickens did for those industries what his corn experiments did for hybrid seed. Wallace, who had encouraged the work of another revolutionary Iowa-born plant scientist, Norman Borlaug, was far from being a communist. Cloudy dreamer and stubborn idealist, perhaps, but no tool of the Soviets.

Still, he was blacklisted from history and died in obscurity. His achievements continue to be under recognized. And his idealism, far from being impractical, is as needed now in these days of presidential incompetence and mendacity as they were in 1944.

Let us end with Studs Terkel's 95th birthday reminiscences and one final thought. "Henry Wallace, he saved the farmers. He saved the camps that were run by the Okies themselves. 'Grapes of Wrath' is all about Henry Wallace's work really. I hope the young have read 'Grapes of Wrath.' The New Deal of Franklin D. Roosevelt and Henry Wallace, it meant jobs, work for men."* Henry Wallace was a man of peace, a man of the people. If only we had him now.

Democracy Now Web site, interview from May 2007.

Jennifer R. Horn

Benediction In Spite Of

There are hazards in practicing
    the art of self-containment,
methodically emptying your pockets of
    the smallest fuzzy remnants
    of any sort of expectation,
keeping hope pushed back
    into the too-small drawer,
    pinched and quietly unruly,
as you walk through your town
    practicing solidity and calling it enough
    practicing living inside the lines of your skin
    practicing liking the lines of your skin
    practicing believing there is sufficient beauty and that
    magic is an untrustworthy itinerant, probably a fiction anyway,
    this is fine, you're fine, this is enough
    and your stride is strong and your back is straight and fine,
then, with another's hand laid on your arm, you're
    suddenly tripped to sprawling in the grass
    with the breath knocked out of you by that
    butterfly bolt of touch
the warmth of contact racing to fill in all the lines in a wing-beat instant,
    face up in a sunlight downpour and without knowing how to breathe in it and, still,
not wanting at all to get up and

walk away from that breathless place
    but knowing it was nothing
    that must be carried home
    where you will add it to the overfull drawer,
    straighten the lines back out,
and resume your practice.

Barbara J. Kalm

Break in the Drought

The cornfield lies face up,
its dry seams open to the sun.
Shriveling corn leaves
point curling spires skyward.

Morning meadows are dry
as old women, and grazing cows
pass confused muzzles over
brown tufts of pasture grass.

Even the pigs, not knowing what
to do stretch in mud hole mirages,
the powdery dirt rising in clouds
above them. Night after night

the farmer and his wife stay up
for the weather, then denounce
the weatherman for telling them
what they already knew.

And day after hot dusty day
they find themselves secretly
making deals, sometimes with God
and sometimes with the devil

about what they would do for
rain, maybe live more honestly
or less honestly, go to church or
even give up religion.

One July night a maverick front
strays down from Canada, lured by
a bedeviling rain man, a full moon
and a small child's prayer.

Quietly it crosses the border
slipping under the color radar,
its low murmuring clouds passing
quickly from county to county.

The first raindrops surprise the
sleeping pigeons, who stir in their
sleep, shift feet and go back
to sleep. The corn leaves rustle and

arch their backs at the disappearing
moon. A sudden downdraft of damp air
passes through the bedroom screen and
brushes the face of the sleeping farmer.

Half asleep, half awake, he stares
unbelieving into the darkness as
he hears the slow advance of rain
over his and his neighbors cornfields.

A slow grin transforms his face
as the frowning face of his banker
fragments in the rain and goes hurrying
down the furrows between the cornrows.

Beverly Johlin

Mustache

His mustach is rich coffee
Blending to creamy latte near the edges.
It's as fluffy as our feather pillow,
Soft, like the well-worn sheets.
After a shower, his mustache is as sleek and shiny
As a harbor seal.
Water droplets cling to its fur.

It brushes hungrily against the muffin
And dips into the milk,
Frosting the 'stache, temporarily.
His mustache nods in agreement
With each of his words,
And fans out, like morning sunrays,
When he smiles.

Denise Tiffany
Mormon Trek Off Benton

The house,
statement of permanence,
imparted confidence.
Dried mud,
scraped off its many visitors' shoes,
clung to the wooden back steps.

When it rained,
we sat under its wide overhang
while Julius Meinl coffee brewed inside.
Her perfect smoke rings rose high, high, high.
Who knew smoke rings could stay round in the rain?

When the call came,
she scratched on the torn scrap
in citu.
I believed myself the teacher:
in situ=on site=where it is.

"What the hell is this," she yelled, waving the corrected message.
"Where else could it be except where it is? Who cares how to spell it?"

She laughed, smoke circles pulsing high, high, high.
She never had a test she couldn't pass.
We all knew she would transcend it,
beat it with laughter; it was only cancer,
after all.

We all knew, despite ribs sticking through her fall sweater,
the cough that punctuated those perfect smoke rings —
scribbling question marks in autumn air.

The house listed; its foundation shifted,
roof askew, climbing weeds constructed
complicated lattices on crumbling walls,
and my friend flat-out died.

The house,
gradually reduced to
undignified piles of splintered boards
and broken bricks,
was one day simply gone,
but for a mud-caked plank
that I imagined for moment
resembled back steps.

M.P. Sarabia

Widow in the Window

■ ■ ■

"I've sold those stock thingies," she waved her arm with the brand of arid dismissal characteristic of an old dog not interested in new tricks — regardless if she had engaged in such tricks the whole of her life and was undoubtedly familiar with them.

"You what? Ma, those stocks were like pure gold," Peter said through a full mouth as he tried to choke down the lukewarm beef stroganoff with its now gelatinized gravy.

"I don't know what to do; I don't have anyone here to help, ack," the whininess in her voice rose to a pitch that threatened to break into sobbing. Peter had hypersensitive awareness of his mother's distress, and was more often than not obliged to smooth it over.

"Ah, ma, you got me. I'm here, aren't I?" He countered with a whine of his own to draw her into understanding — this was how the game worked.

"I know, I know. I just, I don't know about those things"

"But you made a small fortune off them your entire life — you taught me those, those 'things'," he sensed her false incredulity, and with the last words of his sentence let out a sigh, signaling that he had prematurely thrown in the towel. She expected as much.

"Oh, honey. I've no reason to play around with that crap. You do good with it, though," her pithy insulting of his career was always encapsulated in a haphazard euphemism, a euphemism expressed in the same disinterest that allowed for the untimely demise of her beautiful grass, flower garden, and any sense of clothing style she had when courting his father some 40 odd years earlier.

"Yeah," he sat down on her flower-patterned sofa and shoved his hand between the cushions to search for the remote; he could only tolerate a few minutes of her company if the mono speakers on her TV blared with the voice of Bob Barker, or Pat Sajack, or whatever game-show host filled the screen on the only channel of which she claimed to be aware.

She folded her arms across her stomach and said, "I talked to Gladys the other night," she never used specific dates, because that might lead someone — anyone — to suspect that she wasn't decaying with senility.

"Oh yeah? What was she doing," before she could open her mouth, Peter interrupted: "Probably not selling her retirement portfolio"

"Oh Peter, stop it," the arm flailed again. Peter tried to look away each time this happened because the flabby mess attached to her skeletal frame was as graceful in motion as a young gazelle being taken down by a couple of lions.

He tried to prevent himself from insulting her too much, so he humored her roll-of-the-die at trivial conversation, "what'd she have to say?"

"Kids are doing good. That little Miranda consulted with her first broker. Smart little girl she is," she didn't notice her slip until Peter's jaw dropped, and he shut off the television.

"If she's smart, Ma, then what are …. ack. Stop baffling me all this damned time. Why'd you sell the stock? Why, Ma?"

Backed into a corner by the whimsical meanderings of her own pointless conversational musings, the old woman reverted to the age-old excuse all widows are prone to use, "It reminds me too much of your father." It began with a whimper, and as soon as Peter stood up defiantly, threatening to throw a newspaper, throw-pillow, or any other loose item that might afford his frustration a moment of satisfying manifestation, it turned into crying. Peter wasn't going to give in this time, oh no, not this time.

"Stop with this, Ma. You know it's useless to pretend," she looked up at him with the seriousness of a charging bull — still streaming tears — but expression solid as a rock, and mouth pursed like a kid trying to suck all the sweetness out a Jolly Rancher — a look distinctively hers.

"Is that how you view me, then, huh? A liar? A LIAR, Peter? If only your father could hear you say these things, this, this," she was beginning to slip out of her stone-cold demeanor, "this bullshit wouldn't be going on." Peter tilted his eyes and his head, as if these were the only words she said so far that he agreed with — this bullshit wouldn't be happening if his dad were still here, her bullshit in particular.

"Ma, I'm sorry, OK?" She cried and didn't care to give response — the damage had been done, and thus her work finished. "I have to go get the kids. I'll come back later."

"Yeah, uh huh, just, just go, Peter, for God's sake," she shooed him out the door, a rippling-effect in her arm-flab further encouraged him to do so.

Peter reached for the door to his car, which had been freshly repainted recently, when the sprinkler system went off, effectively soaking his silk shirt, pants, and alligator-leather loafers. He threw his arms up in defeat, then turned around to see his Ma, artlessly concealed by the window drapes, peering out at him; the sun's reflection off her coke-bottle glasses gave her position away from a good distance, but he wasn't about to burst her bubble again. She hadn't been, despite years of peering into her neighbor's windows, a covert spy for too long. This battle was hers. Besides, he'd credit the dry cleaning to her account over at McPolly's Cleaners, and she couldn't claim to be aware of what happened.

Molly Shrivert had been manipulating her children like this the whole of their lives. She mastered the art of deception while they still needed training wheels, using her gifts to convince them vacations to Disneyland wouldn't be as fun as those to Vegas, (her art of deception, like many, relied on campaigns of fear) where she could gamble away her alimony, or across country to Maine, where she could deceive another person — her ex-husband, but not father to any of her children — into giving her money. Molly was shrewd, and she thanked God for being so. She knew that by making her neighbors believe the newspaper charged her arbitrary taxes for being the widow of a veteran and thus convincing them to pay for her subscription out their own pocket, or by playing mad-cat games with her children in an effort to divert their attention from the pursuit of her material wealth — she knew that by utilizing her skills of deception and diversion as such stifled the onset of Alzheimer's, her greatest fear.

Molly stepped away from the window and took her hand off the sprinkler-system command module. She pushed two fingers under her scalp and popped off the gray-curled wig, revealing long, wavy brown hair — undeniably dyed — with blond highlights. She walked into the bathroom and continued to undo her age: she removed her coke-bottle glasses, the opaque plastic slips on her teeth that gave them the fake, polished look of dentures, and even some face-putty that had been applied for a wrinkled effect. For a split second, she grinned a Jack Palance grin in the mirror, congratulating her innate deceptive artistry, let slip a witchy chuckle, and pranced into the bedroom; her vibrant, young-looking face appearing awfully odd atop the body of the aging, senile woman we just met, not to mention the skip in her limbs out of tune with the jiggling of fat. She dialed Dolores, her longtime friend and confidant. Though she'd been alive for half as long as Molly, botox and plastic surgery blurred the distance of years, effectively bridging the gap between two or three generations worth of cultural and social evolution. Molly paid no attention to their stark differences though — after all, Marty Robbins and Def Leppard had to have something in common. Dolores couldn't see what, but she let it slide with indeterminable indifference, the same kind that any teenage rock fan had used when the authorities tapped their window, suspecting, upon the window rolling down, that marijuana smoke would billow over and out in a cloud of rebellious haphazardness. Dolores still handled herself like an '80s teenager, clinging to the past with a desperation that, upon observation, would drive a recovering alcoholic back to the bottle for its apparent lack of hope for change. Molly loved this about Dolores, mostly because she was a forty-something version of herself. She had to have someone in line of succession because her own children were the busy-body workaholic types who would age gracefully, and accept the aches, pains, cramps and bewilderment associated with aging. But not Molly — she was going down with a fight. And so was the rubber-cast bodysuit that gave her the appearance of weighing in around 230 pounds. She had been trying to take it off while on the phone, until she told Dolores, "Let me give you a call back, hon," and tossed the phone onto her bed.

The sweat on the inside made the rubbery suit rather viscous, and tore at her arm and leg hairs as she tried to tug it off. There had to be an easier way, there had to be something that would help her get this off. Molly looked all around her house, hopping around while half of the body suit dangled from her dainty limbs. At first she considered the box cutter, but she didn't want to ruin the suit beyond repair. She needed it, usually, once a week for the standard family appearances and get-togethers. She could always buy another, but it might be three to four weeks before CLOWNCO Ltd, manufacturer of a wide-range of entertainment apparel, could have one custom-fit and designed to her specifications. She didn't think Peter could hold off from hounding her for that long. With Vaseline as her only option, Molly yanked a jar out the medicine cabinet, gave it a stiff look, and headed into the bedroom.

Peter always drove cautiously, and of a sound mind. The way in which he turned the wheel, allowing the right angle of pivot on the axle, sent goose bumps up and down his spine. He was proud of his driving skills, and often shared stories of his asphalt-adventures with the water cooler crowd at work; stories that involved his cool demeanor while precisely steering out the way of drunk drivers, or calculating a swerve into an empty lane, thus missing a three-car pile up. He'd always remember the ecstatic, worriless sensation of, through his own disciplined maneuvering, missing an accident and being able to legally drive away without waiting for the cops. Yep, ole' Pete was a dynamo behind the wheel — except when his mother Molly worked him into a crazed frenzy. Those stocks were a sound investment in her retirement, and would have ensured her children a sizeable inheritance. Yeah, so they had the most to benefit from it, probably, but he had warned her of the possibility of needing to enter a convalescent home, and how the extravagant costs of such places would quickly drain any savings she had. The investment would have taken care of that, and then some. Peter had the sneaking suspicion that she covertly funded the research for genetic super-soldiers who would be programmed to storm the city and burn every nursing home and other authority threatening the free will of aging society to the ground. All of this analyzing drove Peter crazy, and made him an angry, offensive driver. He'd been ruthlessly cutting corners, splashing school children with muddy water, cutting people off, gunning it at yellow lights, and taking shortcuts through parking lots going well over 20 mph — all this reckless abandon drove him mad. He needed a diversion, a symbol, a token of something else in his life that was going right.

He remembered the chance encounter with that good-looking mature woman over the weekend. She had seemingly stalked him the whole night across the bar, calculating the speed and trajectory at which she should mount an attack; it was the first time he had ever played the role of the hunted. The memory gave him goose bumps. He flipped down his visor and pulled out a photo of her and Peter that the couple took after a crazy night of drinks and adult activities. His smile slowly stretched to a jaw drop. Staring back at him were those famous pursed lips, doing damage to a world of children's candies.

Peter pulled into the K-Mart parking lot just half a mile away from his Ma's house, kicked open the door, fell out the side of the car, and puked a pile of reheated beef stroganoff into a littered Jack-In-The-Box bag.

William Ford

The Death of a Cat

I put on the paper mask
Against dust and leavings
And sift the litter box
With a plastic scooper
That's full of holes.

My wife and I have cried
Already at how the washer
Slicked clean his bowl
While breaking off
Still another blue chip.

Tonight we'll sleep the sleep
Of partners who find age
A difficult fact anew
When no one else is there
To warm the reaching out.

What's left of the bag
Can be used to leech oil
Off the garage floor,
Give traction in snow
Or drainage to flowers.

Jean Junis
The Obstinate Conception

The moment my mother found out
she was pregnant with me
she almost dropped
her two other babies!
Months later, I was born fast,
almost on the railroad tracks.
The doctor had to be fetched out of church
by the local police.
At the hospital, he swore at my mom,
"You made me miss mass,
godammit!"
Yes, Doctor, puffed my mother.
(What's a woman to say in
such a position?)

At my baptism, the priest
put up a great big fuss, too.
The child's name is not holy enough,
not even a proper saint's name!
He relented, but made my parents
promise to pray extra hard for
my poor little misnamed soul.
Yes, Father, they nodded.
Except, I think they forgot,
with all their babies, and all ...

To tell you the truth,
everyone in this story got real tired.
Bone tired
of trying to tame
wild, pure love —
it can't be done.
But, there's always a lesson
in all good messes.
My parents once whispered it
in my ear,

There are those in this world
who apologize, just for being born!
They beat their breasts when
their sacred name is spoken.

Don't you dare be one of them!

Michael L. McNulty
As I Sit Here Thinking

As I sit here thinking about
Writing about

What I'm thinking about

What I'm thinking about writing
Gets in the way of

Thinking about what
I was thinking about

I spend too much time
Thinking about

What I'm writing
Rather than writing about
What I'm thinking

Mary Joanne Roberts

The Barking Warrior

■ ■ ■

In Yoga class, there is a pose we are asked to assume during every class period. The instructions are, "Take a wide stride with feet facing forward. Turn the right foot out. Bend the right knee not further forward than the ankle. Back leg straight. If needed, take a wider stride. Legs strong. Elevate the arms to shoulder height. Look out over the middle finger of the right hand. Keep those legs strong. Be strong warriors."

The next instructions are basically the same except we turn the left foot out and are careful to bend the left knee no further forward than the ankle. Back legs are urged to be strong and straight. Arms are elevated to shoulder height. We are urged to look out over the middle finger of the left hand. Legs are to be strong and back leg straight.

When I am at home, I pop a tape into the VCR and Suda intones basically the same instructions. When I look out over the middle finger of my right hand, I focus on the light switch on the wall in the bedroom.

Following the directions, I alternate my feet so the left foot is pointed out and the knee is not extended further than my knee. Shoulders are elevated and I gaze out over my left middle finger and focus on the bird feeder tray hanging outside the bedroom window.

Early in the season, it is pleasant to observe the gold finches, house finches, white breasted Nut hatches, Red Bellied wood peckers, red headed woodpeckers, and downy woodpeckers that come to feed every morning. Later in the season is when distraction comes in the form of a fat furry chipmunk, or striped ground squirrel, that amazes me with his ability to climb the shepard's crook that holds the bird feeder. At first, I find it so astonishing, I can only continue with the tape letting the thoughts and mind chatter interfere with my concentration while I contemplate my strategy.

My first act of defense is to spray the pole with my trusty can of non-stick cooking spray. "There," I gloat. "I've got you my nasty little fat bugger" or some rhyming words to that effect.

The next two days are uneventful and I am able to concentrate on my Strong Legs. However, on the third day the slick strategy failed and the nasty little bugger outwitted me again. There he is — gorging himself on the treats, especially the sunflower seeds I put out for my fine feathered friends.

Out comes the non-stick cooking spray for a very dangerously slick coating this time. While I am spraying the pole, I am thinking, "Although we live on a heavily traveled Johnson County road, we are located up on a hill and this is the back of the house, so only those traveling from the north can see me. They will not be able to determine that I am actually applying non-stick cooking spray to the bird-feeder pole."

The summer wears on. My legs are stronger. The chipmunk becomes fatter and fatter.

One morning, in desperation, when I see that fat little bastard gorging himself once more on the goodies in my bird feeder tray, I lose all control and all semblance of maturity.

Taking a line from Clement Moore,

> "Away to the window I fly like a flash.
> Slide open the window"
> And bark like a maniac Chihuahua.

Of course, those actions make one look like a fool. However, no one sees me and miraculous of all, it works. The f.l.b. scurries down the pole and hides under the giant hosta leaves.

Daily I am able to practice my barking skills with the same results. He comes back, I bark vigorously and he runs and hides.

He gorges and I bark.

So we co-exist to fight another day, and another, and another.

in situ

meet the literary and visual artists

Albright, Craig: Chris has an M.F.A. from Indiana University and a B.F.A. from the University of Iowa. His paintings are in the collections of the Figge Art Museum (Davenport), Iowa City Public Library, and numerous private collections throughout the United States. He currently is employed as the pastry manager at New Pioneer Co-op.

Aprile, Tom: Tom is a sculptor and tenured associate professor at the University of Iowa, where he currently is serving as head of the sculpture area. He received his B.F.A from the Cleveland Institute of Art in 1976 and his M.F.A. from Syracuse University in 1978. Tom has been the recipient of many honors and awards including two Pollock/Krasner Foundation Fellowships in 1986 and 1989, a New York Foundation for the Arts Fellowship in 1990, and a Fulbright Scholarship to Nigeria in 1992. Most recently, he was a fellow at the Tyrone Guthrie Centre in County Monaghan, Ireland; and he is currently preparing for a one-person exhibition at the UM Gallery in Seoul, Korea, in fall 2007.

Atkinson, PJM: PJM Atkinson has always been a storyteller. When she was 10 she started writing them down. Now she has reams of paper in almost every genre and medium. She has found that a good writer is merely a conduit. A good story tells itself.

Banning, Shauna: Shauna has always thought herself in some sense a writer. Good, not so good, or great — she writes a little bit of all of it. She is a mother of two full-of-life boys, Vonn and Kingston, and married to a very lucky man, Gregory. She believes her job title will someday read "Best-Selling author and poet." Presently, she is affectionately titled, "Mom."

Batie, Tamara: Tamara is a resident of Iowa City.

Bengtson, Jason: Jason is a graduate student in the Library and Information Science field at the University of Iowa. He's been writing creatively since elementary school and his work is an esoteric mix of nearly every genre.

Bennett, Astrid Hilger: Astrid has been a fiber artist, musician and arts administrator for more than 30 years. An Iowa City resident, Astrid paints and prints all of her own fabrics before quilting them. She exhibits nationally; more about her work can be found on her Web site, www.astrid-hilgerbennett.com.

Birkbeck, John: John was a late bloomer and did not publish any poetry until he was in his mid-40s. Since then he has had poems published in many small-press magazine worldwide, as well as five books of poetry. At present he is the producer and host of a TV show called "The Poets' Corner."

Black, Matt: Matt is 23 and has had an interest in writing from early on in his life. He hasn't been writing much poetry (until somewhat recently) since 2005, instead dabbling in short-fiction and photography. This poem was the first to be reworked and completed since that time.

Blomberg, Carol: As a young girl, Carol loved to write stories, but when she went away to college she ended up in accounting and computer programming. However, she is happy to say that in the last several years, she has once again returned to her childhood love of writing. She looks forward to where this writing journey will lead.

Bolton, Linda: Linda is a writer, a collaborative artist and the daughter of painter Lorraine Williams Bolton. An associate professor of literature and ethics at the University of Iowa, she is the author of "Facing the Other: Ethical Disruption and the American Mind." Linda and public arts sculptor Barbara Grygutis designed and built the second national monument to Martin Luther King Jr. at Battle Creek, Mo.

Bonney, Adele: Adele acquired her writing skills from her experience, with work as varied as paramedic, farmer, psychotherapist and public relations director. A freelancer for the past 20 years, she has developed a specialty in that unique genre: the grant proposal.

Brody, Alan: Alan has a Ph.D. in journalism and mass communication from UI, where he studied Third World Development before joining UNICEF for a 22-year career in international health and social development work. He returned to Iowa City in September 2006 to take up a next career in writing, and to serve his time at manual labor in his wife Mary's flower garden. He studied creative writing as an undergraduate at Yale ('68), and served in the Peace Corps for over seven years.

Campion, Dan: Dan and his wife, JoAnn Castagna, are among the many Iowa Citians who gratefully remember and celebrate the life of David Yerkes. Campion is the author of "Peter de Vries and Surrealism" and coeditor of the anthology "Walt Whitman: The Measure of his Song," and his poetry has appeared in Light, the North American Review, Poetry, Rolling Stone, Shenandoah and other magazines. He is a manager of editorial services at ACT.

Carson, Mary: Mary came to Iowa City in the early 1970s, when windows downtown were boarded from the bricks thrown during anti-war demonstrations. She moved to the country, raised her kids working as a Montessori teacher, getting two more degrees, working at the co-op, then going back to early education. This is home. This is every season to the max. This was heaven, till the hogs.

Charis-Carlson, Jeff: Jeff edits the Press-Citizen Opinion page and is completing a dissertation about novels and stories set in Washington, D.C. He lives in Iowa City with his wife and two daughters.

Cody, Suzanne: Suzanne works at Prairie Lights Books in Iowa City. She also is a student, and single parent to one brilliant girl-child.

Compton, Nick: Nick is a 20-year-old journalism student at the University of Iowa. He writes for Content Magazine and contributes to the Daily Iowan as a sports reporter.

Conley, Garth: Garth lives with his wife and four kids in West Liberty. His painting studio is in West Liberty and he's been painting professionally since 1992. He has self-published a number of prints and has done commissions including portraits locally, across the United States and overseas. He also works in the frame shop at Blick Art Materials downtown.

Cork, Paul: Paul is a 1995 graduate of Iowa State University with a B.F.A. in drawing, painting, and printmaking. After college, he spent seven years working for architectural art class firms in Chicago and Seattle. During that time, he began to formulate a new painting process. Since returning to Iowa in 2002, he has devoted his creative energies to refining his watercolor paintings.

Cox, Howard: Howard is in the health care profession. As a hobby, he enjoys taking pictures of things large and small, and most things in between. He has been taking pictures for a couple of years.

Dallmann, Krissy: Krissy works as a chemist at the University of Iowa Hygienic lab. She pursues her artistic side by writing poems, stories and essays, and also by drawing a cartoon strip of two of her favorite co-workers.

Davis, Patricia: Patricia has enjoyed being a member of the UIRA Gray Hawks Memoirs Writers Group for seven years. She also enjoys music, movies, reading, playing bridge and golf.

Douglas, Andy: Andy has lived in Iowa City since 1993. He recently completed an M.F.A. in non-fiction writing and is working on a book about a spiritual quest in Asia. He also began teaching at the university this fall. He can be seen walking in various city parks with his black lab, Pete, who is almost 15 years old.

Feldstein, Peter: Peter received his M.A. and M.F.A in art from the University of Iowa. He taught courses in photography and digital imaging in the School of Art and Art History for 32 years. He has exhibited nationally for 40 years and has received grants from the National Endowment for the Arts and the Polaroid Corporation. He is now retired and living in Oxford.

Fitzpatrick, Julie: Painting became a part of Julie's life six years ago thanks to the encouragement of her life partner. She is self-taught and continues to learn through observation and interaction with other artists, as well as by trial and experimentation. In addition to painting, she enjoys interior design and has her own business, Indigo Interiors; however, her professional training is in physical therapy, and she currently serves as the chief operating officer for Premier Health Associates.

Ford, William: William has published two books of poems, "The Graveyard Picnic" (Mid-America Press, 2002) and "Past Present Imperfect" (Turning Point, 2006), taught at the University of Iowa, Coe College, and Kirkwood Community College, and now is retired. He and his wife have lived in Iowa City since 1983, most recently in the Sherwood Forest area behind Mayflower.

Gantz, Bernice: Bernice's love for the arts started when she was a youngster. She attended Pratt Institute in New York. This solidified her desire to go into watercolors, which is her chosen medium.

Gruenhaupt, Fran: Writing stories about Fran's early life on her family's Century Iowa Farm helped ease the sense of loss she felt when the farmstead was sold. She began writing five years ago after joining a writing class at the Senior Center, and she now enjoys recording those stories for her seven grandchildren. Jean was a nursing home administrator before retiring and moving to Iowa City seven years ago.

Hahn, Adam: Adam has been an Iowa City-based writer and performer for the better part of the last decade. He also is a student in the summer M.F.A. playwriting program at Hollins University in Roanoke, Virginia.

Hershberger, Sue: Sue works at the University of Iowa and lives eight miles southwest of Iowa City on a farm with her husband, Nelson. She isan amateur photographer and took this picture during a morning walk last summer.

Hinton, Howard, Jr.: Howard's goal is to capture vivid images that keep memories and visions alive for a lifetime. He is co-owner of Reminders Plus Photography and a long time member of the Iowa City Camera Club. He has been involved with photography for the past 20 years.

Horn, Jennifer R.: Jennifer is a native Midwesterner and is happy to have landed in Iowa City, such a rich place for art with words and without words. She's most honored to have been able to help give naming words to her daughters, and she's thankful for the Barcalounger Cowboys of St. Columcille's, which is the best sort of writers' group a person could dream up.

Hubel, Kenn: Kenn retired eight years ago as a physician-teacher at the College of Medicine. Walking each morning with a camera in hand, he documents the seasonal appearance of the flowers, learns their names and looks for the unusual in the ordinary. A small miracle compounded of chemistry, physics and optics, that precious instrument has documented his 80 years of living and provides continuing retrospective pleasure for himself and those he loves.

Jacobsen, Cheryl: Cheryl is a freelance lettering artist and adjunct professor for the University of Iowa's Center for the Book. She has been working extensively and creatively with letters for over 20 years. She is also known as Sophie and Julia's mom.

Johlin, Beverly: Although Beverly enjoys writing poetry and travel journals, her favorite form is the novel. She currently is trying to publish her seaside mystery "The Breaking of a Wave," plus she is busy composing the second book of the series.

Junis, Jean: Jean has enjoyed reading and writing poetry for years, and is now beginning to share her poems. She resides in Iowa City, where she teaches young children how to read and write.

Kalm, Barbara: Barbarba is a native Iowan, retired University Hospitals nurse, mother, grandmother, avid gardener and sometimes poet. Her father loved poetry and read it to her as a child — it stuck.

Kaune, Melinda: Currently working as a graphic designer, Melinda received a B.F.A. with a graphic design emphasis from the University of Iowa in 2005. Having an interest in photography for 10 years, she also enjoys oil painting and charcoal drawing. Graphic design has refined her artistic eye and opened a new avenue to digital mediums.

Kehoe, Tonya E.: Tonya is an assistant professor of art at Kirkwood Community College — Iowa City campus. She graduated from the University of Iowa with a master's in art and art education in 1997. She teaches painting, design and art appreciation.

Kellenberger, Gordon: Gordon is a full-time pastel painter working out of the Wasch Haus Studio in High Amana, Iowa, one of the seven historic villages of the Amana Colonies. Gordon is a past recipient of the Iowa Arts Council's Iowa Arts Award, which honors individuals for their commitment to excellence in the arts. His pastels are found in many private and public collections throughout the United Sates.

Kilgore, Chris: Chris is 29 and a student at the University of Iowa. He was born and raised in Dubuque, Iowa, and has lived in Iowa City for about 10 years. He thinks he's been writing stories about as long as he's been able to write.

Knox, Patricia: Patricia has been a studio artist working as a metalsmith, contemporary jewelry designer and sculptor for more than 25 years. Some of her other interests include international relations and architectural design and remodeling. She serves on the board of the Council for International Visitors to Iowa Cities and the Friends of Cedar Rock, the Usonian home by Frank Lloyd-Wright in Quasqueton, Iowa. She lives in Iowa City.

Krieger, Jan: Jan grew up on a farm in Henry County with her parents and nine sisters. She returned to her native rural Iowa land with her partner and two children to share her love of the land. Krieger's favorite subjects remain the people she alone has access to — her family. Jan takes a direct approach of photographing. Her prints reveal the earthy, poignant and beautiful private moments shared. The photograph included in this book is of her daughter, Emma, at 11 years old, who has discovered the beauty of living on the land.

Lance, Phyllis: Phyllis received her B.A. in art at the University of Iowa in 1954 and has participated in the world of art ever since. She has done ceramics, metalsmithing, weaving, printmaking, oil painting and now is concentrating on watercolor.

Lim, Ramon: Ramon is Professor Emeritus of Neurology at the University of Iowa. He is a professional calligrapher whose works are represented at Chait Galleries Downtown. He is vice president of the Chinese Calligraphy Association of the Rocky Mountain region and a winner of the International Calligraphy Competition in Shanghai in 2005. Trained in abstract painting, he expresses the abstract beauty of the ancient Chinese art of calligraphy from the esthetic perspectives of Western modern art.

Lyvers, Matt: Matt is 35 years old and has lived in the Iowa City area for about 25 years. He has dabbled in art for as long as he can remember, but in the last 8 to 10 years he has really began tapping into his creative side and applying it to his art. He has worked with different mediums through the years, but recently has become fond of working with pastels and is looking forward to working with different mediums in the future.

McCue, Patrick: Patrick grew up attending Regina elementary and high school in Iowa City, and currently is a sophomore at Montana State University in Bozeman studying physical therapy. Through grade school, he was always told he wrote well, but he did not embrace it and begin writing for himself until two years ago.

McFarlane, L. Ward: L. Ward McFarlane is originally from Northeast Iowa. Like so many others, she came to the University of Iowa as a student and ended up staying longer than planned. So far about 20 years longer, and she still resides in Iowa City with her family. She has dabbled with writing fiction since she was a pre-teen and prefers to add an Iowa flavor to most of her stories.

McNulty, Michael L.: Michael was born and raised in western Pennsylvania, and is married to Darlene and has two children, Shannon and Sean, and four grandchildren, Mikayla, Deklin, Quinlan and Carson. He is emeritus professor of geography and former associate provost and dean for International Programs at the University of Iowa. He recently joined the Gray Hawks Memoir Writers Group and enjoys the opportunity to share experiences and sharpen his writing skills with other members.

McNutt, Jeff: Jeff is a native Iowan, a past Herky the Hawk mascot and has been painting since 1992. He began creating Iowa Hawkeye paintings in 2005 by using oil paint and recycling brick, metal and wood from Kinnick Stadium on canvas. He currently lives in Iowa City with his wife, Beth, and two sons, Carter and Sawyer.

Meister, Nick: Nick has been painting in watercolor for 10 years. He absolutely loves the flow and unpredictability of the medium. There aren't enough watercolor artists being taken seriously.

Mendenhall, JD: JD is a writer, humorist, freelancer and newspaper columnist who began his second career as a professional writer in 1998 with a bi-weekly humor and observation column for Icon, Iowa City's independent, alternative newspaper. Since 2004, he has written a monthly column as a Iowa City Press-Citizen Writers' Group member. He also is a marketing writer for Stamats Communications Inc. in Cedar Rapids. He lives with his wife, Janis, and their daughter, Kate, in Iowa City.

Messier, Jason: Jason is a full-time graduate student at the University of Iowa Metals program and a part-time mechanic in Coralville. He grew up in the country around classic cars and motorcycles, in which both have played a major role in the art he creates. His personal goal is to get your not-so-typical collectors interested in fine art by offering something completely different

Miller, Liz Lynn: Liz's poems have recently appeared in publications such as Cimarron Review, Main Channel Voices, My Favorite Bullet, and I Typed For Miles. Her poems also occasionally appear, one at a time and with suitable visuals, as postcards, greeting cards or fliers for the amusement of friends. In her spare time, between writing and hanging with all her favorite people, she works at an Iowa City elementary school.

Muehl, Lois: Writing in her spare time has been a longtime pleasure for Lois. At first it produced children's stories and domestic articles when she was a stay-at-home mom with four moppets, then professional articles and a textbook while she taught rhetoric and ran the Reading Lab at the University of Iowa. Now in retirement, she's free to bounce from poetry and light verse to short prose — and she does. One side benefit: Participating in writing groups has brought her many fascinating friends.

Neumann, Zak: Zak was born and raised in West Branch. Now living in Iowa City, he's been taking photos since he was a sophomore in high school and has since taken classes at Kirkwood Community College in photography, printmaking and other media.

Noethen, Brittany: Brittany is an artist living in a technology manager's body. She would rather be decapitated than give up making art, trading atcs. or stop thinking that the phrase "Muffins or Bust" is hilarious. She currently lives in Iowa City with her partner Cat, her dog of 12 years Maggie and shelves full of art supplies.

Norberg, Frederik: Born in Chicago, raised in the cornfields of Chariton, Iowa, Fred ventured to Iowa City in 1980 and has been a resident ever since. Actor, playwright and soldier of fortune, Fred plies his crafts in the education trade, while taking time off to share food and movies with friends. The phrase, "Oh, what a day!" is often heard coming from his lips.

Petrick, Joseph M.: Joseph wrote this bio about himself and can't help but feel somewhat silly. Nevertheless, he proceeds with vigor. He is 25 years old and has worked a total of 12 different jobs paying minimum wage, four of them as a convenience store clerk. He loves his cat, Nelson, old Billy Wilder movies and the plaid piece at beginning of the tape roll. According to his mother, he is the most handsome boy in the whole world and any woman would be lucky to have him.

Phillips, Dale: Dale learned photography in school; not photography school-school. She developed an eye for balance, color, simplicity and beauty while taking pictures of teachers and children during her 30-year career as an educational consultant. She owes her first photography "lessons" with a second-hand 35 mm SLR to her husband, Darrell." When she retired on disability, photography became a blessing and therapy. She finds "treasure"— plants, people, animals and even "beautiful junk" — in small, undisturbed natural "vignettes." She doesn't rearrange anything and doesn't like doing "computer magic." Sixty-two year-old Dale is excited that this is her first juried photo publication.

Radl, Sophie: Sophie currently is a student at Kirkwood Community College studying art and Spanish. She's still deciding what she's going to do for a living, but black and white photography, painting and sewing are her hobbies. She plans to stay at Kirkwood for a couple years and then transfer to the University of Iowa. She's big on traveling, and she hopes to study Spanish abroad for a semester or two.

Roberts, Connie: Connie is a graduate of the University of Iowa with a master's and M.F.A., both in painting. She has been making her living as a sculptor, doing things like this for nearly 20 years and having them sold nationally as well as locally (Iowa Artisans Gallery) Her husband paints full time and both daughters also are artists.

Roberts, Elizabeth: Elizabeth comes from an entire family of artists, so it is in her blood. She is obsessed with the human figure, especially the figure she sees every day — her own. Call it narcissistic if you like, she only sculpts what she sees and loves.

Roberts, Mary Joanne: Mary Joanne is a retired special education teacher. He last position was with a special education co-op in Illinois. She and her husband, a former superintendent of schools in Iowa and Illinois, retired to a farm that has been in his family since 1867 in western Johnson County. They do not farm but rent the farmland and spend their days volunteering at the Crisis Center Food Bank and as small claims mediators in Johnson County Courts. They travel; winter in Tucson where she is a member of a writing workshop group.

Rude, Jean Murphy: Jean formerly worked in advertising, writing and producing television and radio spots. She began writing poetry at the age of 11. Currently, she is home with her children and enjoys attending with her family the many cultural events in Iowa City.

Sarabia, Michael: Michael is a student of law, lover of literature, and disciple of nothing; a dilettante of life and a master of pursuits. He is a firm believer in guidance through naivety, and attempts to implement this belief in his own life as far as is practicable. In his spare time, he rummages through collections of unused witticisms as a cure for his lack of character.

Scarth, Linda and Robert: Linda and Robert have been active in this medium for many years. They work to present the natural world in ways that encourage viewers to pay more attention to the beauty, fragility, resilience and power of nature on earth. In doing so, they hope that people are motivated to care and protect the places in which they live.

Seager Frerichs, Dannye: Dannye lives in Iowa City with her husband and three children. Her first novel, "Bloodchild," was published in 2002. Currently she writes romances under the name "Dannye Chase."

Sharp, Barry: Barry grew up in Bettendorf on the banks of the Mississippi River, watching the passing of trains, riverboats and barges, which instilled the wanderlust at an early age. He has traveled extensively to 49 of the 50 country's states. He has always been amazed at the great diversity of the United States, inspiring him to capture it through his photography. He shoots primarily portrait and landscape photography. He is the director/CEO of an Iowa City hospital and is a resident of Solon.

Smith, Nick: Nick is a teacher at the Highland Community School District. He loves teaching English and finds every day to be both rewarding and exciting. His wife also is a teacher, and he has three children and eight grandchildren. It's all a riot!

Stanley, Corinne: Corinne is presently working on a memoir, "Daughter of Corn: A Woman's Journey from Iowa to Mexico." She previously translated for the IWP at the University of Iowa and has just completed a poetry collection, "Breathe into the Knowing."

Starke, Jonathan: Jonathan graduated from the University of Iowa in 2006 with a BA in English and hopes to someday earn an M.F.A. in creative writing. The works of John Steinbeck and Raymond Carver have long been influential to his writing as well as the encouragement of his mentor and dear friend, Thomas Simmons.

Starr Ryan, Alicia: Alicia received her B.F.A, M.A. and M.F.A. from the University of Iowa School of Art and Art History. Her work has been exhibited in New York, Kansas City and Chicago. She is currently working as a graphic designer at the Iowa City Press-Citizen.

Strating, Jason "Ja" S.: As long as Jason can remember, art has been a part of his life. As a young boy growing up in Florida, he has vivid memories of exploring the world of color. He went on to study the world of photography in Chicago and worked in a commercial photography studio, where he learned to see the world in a different light. He relocated to Iowa City in 2000. He spent several years learning and performing the art of tattooing. He has photographed and designed posters and CD covers for local musicians as well as publicity designs for community theater productions. Currently, he is working on a series of paintings as an exploration of self.

Stukel, Mindy: Mindy is a full-time nursing student attending Kirkwood Community College working her way toward nurse anesthetist. She's also a full-time mom to four beautiful children and a full-time unit clerk/CNA at Mercy Hospital. Photography is her hobby and she's been taking photographs off and on since 1984. Only recently did she become far more involved with it and plans to take some more courses in photography at Kirkwood.

Tenold, Gerine: Gerine was born Sept. 25, 1949. She was a gentle soul who loved the literary field and all it had to offer. After working for more than two decades at Louis Rich Foods in West Liberty and struggling with night classes, she quit her job to go to school full time. She graduated from the University of Iowa in 1999 with a B.A. in English. A new career was not to be, as Gerine was overcome by breast cancer in December 2001. Psychedelia is submitted to showcase her remarkable talent.

The Bomb Shaman: "When everything went grey, my blindness returned and transformation became impossible. Again left with my only cadence: SUBMISSION=TRANSGRESSION."

Thompson, Helen: Helen is 23-year-old University of Iowa student and mother of two. She graduated from Kirkwood in Cedar Rapids last year and is majoring in law and political science.

Tiffany, Denise: Denise is an Iowa City writer and teacher.

Tomanek, Rita Svoboda: Rita received her B.F.A. in studio art from the University of Iowa and has exhibited her painting, mixed media, sculpture and photography throughout Iowa. She developed the Art Cart program within Project Art at University Hospitals. Her artwork draws from her experiences as a hospice and church volunteer, chaplain, masseuse, mother, grandmother and gardener.

Ulmer, Spring: Spring received her B.F.A. from the Cooper Union School of Art and her M.F.A. in poetry from the University of Arizona. She worked as a journalist in Eastern Kentucky and is the author of "Benjamin Spectacles," a book of poetry selected by Sonia Sanchez for Kore Press's 2007 First Book Award.

Vermillion, Mary: Mary is a professor of English at Mount Mercy College in Cedar Rapids and the author of two mystery novels. Her second one, "Murder by Mascot," is set in Iowa City, where she has lived for 21 years.

Wahls, Terry L., M.D.: Terry is an internal medicine physician, working at the VA and University Hospitals. In addition to practicing and teaching medicine, she is a writer. Her current project is a memoir, which provides a glimpse into medicine, parenthood and being diagnosed with progressive multiple sclerosis.

Wegman, Marcia: Marcia has lived in Iowa City for 50 years, having come here to graduate school in the art department in 1957. For 34 years, she was one of the owners of Things & Things & Things in downtown Iowa City. Currently her work is landscapes in dry pastel, most of which depict Johnson County.

Welsh, Kathryn: Kathryn is the mother of two children and married to Bartley Brown. She is an adjunct instructor of English as a Second Language at Kirkwood Community College.

Whitters, Andrew: Andrew works and enjoys his duties as a cardiovascular operating room nurse at Mercy Hospital in Iowa City. He considers himself a lifelong learner in his profession and he is pursuing studies as a graduate nursing student. Caring for people as a nurse has always been his first passion next to being a husband and now expecting father. He and his wife have lived in Iowa City for nearly three years. He has worked in the arts as a hobbyist photographer and ceramicist since he was a kid.

Woito, Linda Newman: Linda, a semi-retired attorney, likes to spend time with grandsons Ian and Leo and to write poetry, which appears in Poetry NZ, Wisconsin People & Ideas, Main Street Rag, Free Verse, The Rockford Review, Prairie Winds, and Sweet Annie Review.

Wyrick, Shirley: Shirley is an Iowa City artist whose major sculptural works for public viewing are located at the C. Maxwell Stanley Hydraulics Laboratory Building, the Levitt Center for University Advancement, the University of Iowa's Blank Honors Center and the Johnson County Administration Building in Iowa City; the State of Iowa Historical Building in Des Moines; and the Regency West Office Park in West Des Moines. She also has had several solo exhibitions of her drawings and smaller-scale sculptures in the Midwest and has work in private collections in the U.S. and Europe. Her M.A. and M.F.A. degrees in art were earned in the 1970s from the University of Iowa.

Young, Laura: Laura is currently a lecturer in the School of Art and Art History at the University of Iowa. She has won many grants and fellowships and holds degrees from Skidmore College, Montclair State University and Rutgers University and has been represented in museum and gallery shows nationally and internationally.

Zollo, Rick: Rick has M.F.A.s from the Writer's Workshop in fiction and creative nonfiction. For the past 10 years, he has been a staff writer at Buckledown Publishing in Iowa City.